Cultures in Motion

Cultures in Motion

Mapping Key Contacts
and Their Imprints in World History

Peter N. Stearns

Yale University Press
New Haven and London

11/17/01

Published with assistance from the Kingsley Trust Association Publication Fund
established by the Scroll and Key Society of Yale College.

Designed by Miryan Kenet.
Set in Century type by Kenet Books.
Printed in the United States of America.

Library of Congress Cataloging-in-Publication Data
Stearns, Peter N.
    Cultures in Motion : mapping key contacts and their imprints in world history /
    Peter N. Stearns.
        p. cm.
    Includes bibliographical references and index.
    ISBN 0-300-08228-2 (cloth : alk. paper) — ISBN 0-300-08229-0 (pbk. : alk. paper)
    1. Civilization—History. 2. Acculturation—History. I. Title.
    CB151 .S75 2001
    909—dc21   2001033314

A catalogue record for this book is available from the British Library.

The paper in this book meets the guidelines for permanence and durability
of the Committee on Production Guidelines for Book Longevity of the Council on
Library Resources.

10 9 8 7 6 5 4 3 2 1

Contents

Acknowledgments

Marc Kolc, Clio Stearns, and particularly Halil Damar provided indispensable and imaginative research assistance on this book. Darlene Scalese and Sarah Thompson shepherded the manuscript. Brian Kenet spurred the idea in the first place. My sincere thanks to all.

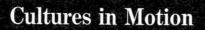

Cultures in Motion

Introduction

This is a book about contacts between cultures as a theme in world history since the beginning of civilization. Examples of these cultural contacts, and their resulting influences and impacts, are abundantly familiar in our own age. Christian evangelical missionaries from Western Europe, and even more often the United States, bring their message to Russia, whose government in 1997 tried to limit their operations. Missionary efforts have also generated one of the most important cultural changes in Latin America in recent decades: the spread of Protestant fundamentalism. The export of McDonald's restaurants to Europe, Asia, and Russia challenges traditional food choices and eating patterns—and the restaurants' success both causes and reflects important changes in values. Women's magazines in India debate the impact of Hollywood images of romantic love on a culture where arranged marriage is customary. And important influences run in other directions—to the West as well as from it—in modern times. In the 1980s, American companies were urged to imitate Japanese corporate culture, which emphasized group harmony and mutual consultation.

Current patterns of cultural contact have not always prevailed, to be sure. Western Europe and the United States became predominant sources of international influence only in recent centuries. Prior to 1600, the most significant contacts involved influences from Asia and parts of Africa. The pace of cultural interaction has accelerated in modern times, with growing world trade and advanced communications technology. Still, the theme of contact stretches far into the past. China imported Buddhism from India about seventeen hundred years ago; even earlier, artists in India were representing Hindu gods in the costumes of the Greeks because of a brief but intense exchange with the armies of Alexander the Great.

Cultural contact looms large in world history for two related reasons. First, it provides moments of obvious drama. What messages would American Indians take from their encounters with European conquerors and missionaries after literally millennia of developing beliefs and artistic styles in isolation? How would the Japanese, long and justly proud of their distinctive culture, manage to import Western European and American science and education in the late nineteenth century without losing their cultural pride and identity? Second, contact provides one of the great forces of change in world history. Western European philosophical and scientific development could not have proceeded as it did, from the eleventh century onward, without borrowing from Islamic scholarship (amid intense hatred and fear of Islam itself). Nationalism, one of the motivating loyalties of modern world history, was a product of cultural contact with Western Europe—ironically both facilitating and impeding exchange.

In this book I present a number of case studies of cultures in motion, from early civilization to the present. My goal is to explore important contacts, with maps and other materials, rather than to provide a comprehensive survey. In studying several key episodes of cultural contact, of cultures in geographic motion, I depend on two basic definitions—first, of culture, and second, of the circumstances surrounding contact—to understand why contact usually involves significant challenge and controversy.

A society's culture involves its basic beliefs and values and the styles and methods used to express those beliefs and values. Human beings require elaborate belief systems because, as a species, our inherent instincts are fairly modest. We do not need culture to teach us to recoil from fire or to breastfeed a child, but we do need beliefs or assumptions to tell us what kinds of families to form or how to deal with death or whether the sun will return amid the darkness of winter. Reliance on culture rather than on instinct helps people adapt to a variety of situations—for a complex species, humans are amazingly adaptive to different environments. But the same reliance means that a range of belief systems can develop from one region to the next. Sometimes cultures can even prompt a denial of instinct, as when societies come to believe that breastfeeding is ugly or unhealthful and turn to some other method of feeding infants.

Cultures initially developed in considerable isolation. During the long hunting and gathering phase of human history, people had to fan out over wide geographic areas. By 10,000 BCE, on the eve of the invention of agriculture, there were perhaps 10 million people in the whole world, but they stretched over virtually all the inhabitable territory. Bands of hunters and gatherers, with about eighty people in each band, had contacts with each other, of course. But bands in one region might develop very different beliefs from those of bands in the next. They could vary in spoken language (which reflects assumptions and also constrains beliefs), ideas about particular gods and objects in nature, or understanding of what happens after death. Identities developed among regional groups on the basis of their beliefs, as did an understanding that other regions had different beliefs and styles (and, it was often assumed, inferior ones).

Isolation was never complete because the human species has so often depended on migrations and because the impulse to develop trading contacts developed so early. Some of the initial contacts involved the wanderings of successive humanoid species, usually from Africa into Asia and Europe, but also from Asia to the Americas and to Australia and the Pacific islands. Later migrations not only spread the species geographically, they also allowed contact with technological advances, ultimately including agriculture itself. And there were doubtless cultural implications as well: people could learn new religious beliefs or art forms through contact, though precise evidence of what ideas were exchanged is often lacking. Still, while recognizing interaction as a human constant, it is also important to note the extent to which early societies established space for distinctive emphases. Even societies maturing relatively close together, like Egypt and the Middle East after 3500 BCE, and sharing periodic contact through trade and war, generated very different religions, art forms, and even basic inclinations toward optimism or pessimism. Differences of these sorts could make subsequent contact both fruitful and disturbing.

A major part of human history since the hunting and gathering phase has involved contact between one regional culture and the next. The development of agriculture, starting about 9000 BCE, encouraged contact in at least two senses. First, many agricultural peoples generated expanding populations (birth rates went up with the advent of agriculture), and these sought to fan out to other areas, where they could displace or merge with existing peoples. Wars over territory among neighboring regions were a specific form of this process. Second, most agricultural societies developed some surplus and specialization, which encouraged trade—and this inherently generated contact. Sometimes, contact was so extensive that two cultures fused into one, creating larger cultural zones. Civilizations, particularly from the classical period onward, resulted from this process of integrating cultures into larger units, such as China or India. Often, however, cultural interaction fell short of full merger but involved important mutual influence.

Contact between two cultures could be momentous, precisely because differences were often great. From contact, religious or scientific ideas could spread; artists could seize on different styles. Or a culture could pull back, seeking to reduce interaction and preserve existing values, but this also would be a change in its own right. Some cultural contact was entirely accidental, the result of war, invasion, or trade—though it might be welcomed even so. Some contact, however, could be deliberately sought, as when one society set about imitating aspects of a neighboring culture. A key variation involved a given culture's degree of openness to the outside world. Some societies, often because of experience, developed a habit of considering other beliefs and styles and selecting features that might be incorporated with existing traditions. Others developed an impulse to resist influences of this sort. The array of reactions to contact was considerable, from the early stages of world history onward.

Much of the stuff of world history, indeed, involves looking at how societies deal with cultural opportunities—whether they seek them, adjust if compelled, or actively resist. And of course reactions change over time. At the beginning of the twenty-first century, for example, many major societies profess some willingness to learn from other cultures, but a number of reactions have developed against too much porousness, in favor of real or imagined religious or national traditions. A key means of understanding current cross-cultural influences and sensitivities involves looking at past patterns.

Contacts among people with well-established patterns of beliefs and styles began early, as we have seen, simply because people have so often been mobile. In world history, assessment of extensive contacts becomes easier with the formation of early civilizations along key river valleys in Asia and Africa, from 3500 BCE onward.

Civilizations were typically larger than most previous culture zones. They usually boasted greater surpluses in agriculture, which allowed the formation of more extensive cities and also more pronounced social inequality. They had formal governments. These characteristics often involved more explicit (sometimes government-directed) efforts to spread a common culture within the civilization and also to insist on its differences from the beliefs and styles of other societies. Civilization, in other words, affected the process of contact, making it in some ways more challenging. At the same time, many people long remained outside civilizations; nomadic groups, particularly, developed important beliefs and institutions of their own and also helped assure that civilizations avoided complete isolation as they moved among borders.

During the classical period of world history, which began after 1000 BCE, several civilizations worked hard to spread coherent cultures over wider areas—China, India, and the Mediterranean. Contact among these larger cultures was rare but potentially extremely important. After the great classical empires declined, mostly by the fifth century CE, more extensive cultural interactions developed, particularly because of the spread of missionary religions—Buddhism, Christianity, and Islam—and because of the development of more regular international trading networks. Various kinds of cultural contact accelerated during this postclassical period. From 1450 to 1750 CE—the early modern period of world history—a number of societies pulled back from contact, but others were subjected to new and often unwelcome influences from the outside. Interaction among American, European, and African cultures was a vital new ingredient in world history. Between 1750 and the early twentieth century, new technologies in transportation and communication, plus growing Western European power in the world at large, prompted most societies to consider what to do about the cultural example of Western Europe. Finally, in the twentieth century, even more massive changes in communication and trade, plus complex reshufflings of power balances, redefined the issue of cultural contact once again.

Cultural contact, in sum, has gone through a number of iterations, depending on international trade patterns, relevant technology, and simple eagerness or reluctance to spread beliefs. In this book I present key episodes of contact with a brief definition of each successive chronological period. Culture—what people believe, and what their beliefs prompt them to do—is one of the most fascinating aspects of the human species and its long history. Precisely because cultures provide identity, and often prompt resistance to change in the name of established assumptions, consideration of the diverse impacts of cultural meetings provides a key to larger processes in world history.

Three final points. First, in this book I do not deal with all important cases of cultural contact, even after the earlier periods of human history. Instead I select key instances in which belief systems (religious or political or consumerist) spread widely. This allows an understanding of the process of cultural contact, which can be applied to other examples as well—whether historical or contemporary. Second, the cases that are pursued make it clear that cross-cultural contact has complex results that can be diversely evaluated.

Contacts bring new ideas, which can be immensely creative and liberating. But they also can undermine precious traditions and identities. This helps explain why contacts often bring unexpected and sometimes vicious reactions, and also why many people, in the societies affected, legitimately wonder whether they might not have been better off had they been left alone. The chapters that follow allow analysis of these diverse results, along with appreciation for human ingenuity in projecting combinations of cultural influences. Finally, cultural contact often occurs amid societies of unequal power. This can make one culture seem "superior"—which really means that its ideas and styles are associated with particular military or economic success, not that they are in principle truer or more beautiful. Tracing the power ramifications of cultural contact is a vital part of the analysis. This is true in civilization's early period, and also as what is sometimes called Western civilization (the civilization that developed in Western Europe and then spread to an extent to places like the United States) grew ascendant. But again, complexity: cultures that are superior in terms of power rarely triumph fully, even when their leaders believe they have won; and even "superior" cultures are affected by the ideas with which they have contact.

Part I
Early Cultural Contacts Through the Classical Period

From the time that human beings had speech and ideas about nature and death—at least 100,000 years ago—they were capable of spreading beliefs and styles. Early cultural contacts and diffusion are shrouded in mystery because there are no direct, written sources that spell out value systems of the time. Scholars believe that they can trace, in modern languages, some kinds of dissemination. Certain word relationships—for example, between the word for "fist" and the related word for "five"—suggest original languages, long since gone, from which a host of tongues now current in Asia and Europe all derive. Another intriguing clue involves common stories. Peoples from Siberia to Europe, for example, have a story about defeating evil through use of a shoe; in Europe, this story appeared as the tale of Cinderella, which of course passed with Europeans to the Americas. Some argue that these common story bases were brought from one area to the next by nomads.

With the development of agriculture (in 9000 BCE) and civilization as a form of human organization (from 3500 BCE), cultural contact becomes more traceable. Civilizations systematized ideas into organized stories, philosophies, and formal religions, and they also began to record key concepts. Civilizations spread common belief patterns over wider areas as a means of linking diverse peoples. Civilizations, finally, could have formal contact with one another, providing mutual cultural influence. This section deals with various types of cultural contact in the early millennia of civilizations in Asia, North Africa, and southern Europe. In the first chapter, on cultural contacts over geographic space, I discuss contact between southern Europe and two of the earliest areas with civilizations, in the Middle East and in Egypt, and questions about the resulting influences on Greek styles in art, mathematics, and other areas. Direct interaction between Greek and Indian civilizations offers the first instance in which it is possible to trace a more formal, though temporary, exchange of ideas. The cultural experience of an exceptionally coherent people, whose wanderings through Africa, Asia, Europe, and ultimately the Americas

proved extensive, offers a different kind of example of contact and preservation, hence the chapter on the Jewish diaspora, which would continue into later periods and up to modern times.

The establishment of formal religions that not only claimed truth—which the Jewish religion had already done, as had many polytheistic religions—but also vowed to convert nonbelievers ushered in a major pattern of cultural contact and dissemination. The two earliest religions to attempt a deliberate missionary effort were Buddhism and Christianity. Their wide geographical impact began during the classical period but, like the travels of the Jews, extended into later centuries as well.

In this section I deal with early civilizations, in which writing, statecraft, and other important markers first arose, and with the classical civilizations that emerged, after the initial civilization period in China, India, and the Mediterranean, between 1000 BCE and 450 CE. Classical civilizations were larger than those of their antecedents, most of which had clustered around river valleys. As a result of their size, the classical civilizations worked harder to develop cultural systems that would help integrate extensive territories. The first missionary religions arose during the classical period, sometimes to dispute prior cultural systems—as Buddhists disagreed with some aspects of Hinduism in India—but always to try to spread ideas beyond their original centers, using the trade routes and political institutions that the classical civilizations provided as a framework for new contacts and combinations.

1. Egypt and the Middle East: The Contact with Early Greece

The great river-valley civilizations of the Middle East and Egypt unquestionably spread cultural influences beyond their normal borders. Egyptians, for example, interacted with sub-Saharan African people along the Upper Nile, helping to form the Kush civilization and then its successors. There have been claims that the range of Egyptian and Middle Eastern influence extended to the Iberian Peninsula, southern Russia, and India, but there is little evidence for such claims, beyond occasional trade routes for artifacts and crafts. Greece and the Aegean islands form a different story. Here, contacts began early and were undeniably extensive. Greeks looked to the Middle East and Egypt as cultural ancestors even as they proudly asserted their own identity.

Debate flourishes in this case as well. Not about contact itself, for there is ample evidence that Greece borrowed extensively from its two more advanced neighbors during the second millennium BCE and beyond. The question is: How much was borrowed, and in what spirit? In the 1990s Martin Bernal advanced the idea that most of the main ingredients of Greek culture, including its emphasis on mathematics and philosophical inquiry, were simply imports, and that the Greeks almost deliberately downplayed their debt. Attacking the many historians who have heaped praise on the Greek legacy, Bernal contends that the Greeks get too much credit for originality and imagination, which really should go to Africans and Middle Easterners. His claims have been vigorously slammed by other scholars, who accept influence but not wholesale importation. The problem is compounded by other evidence. We know that Greeks looked up to the Egyptians but that they also regarded them as strange in many ways, judging by travel accounts by such people as the historian Herodotus. There is no clear attribution of major philosophical notions to Egypt, and no clear connecting evidence. So the debate continues.

What is undeniable, however, is that several exchange points did exist during the heyday of the Middle East and Egypt, and that Greeks borrowed extensively but also combined the influences with local features in

Bronze Age Trade Routes (c. 1450 BCE)

⟶ Trade routes

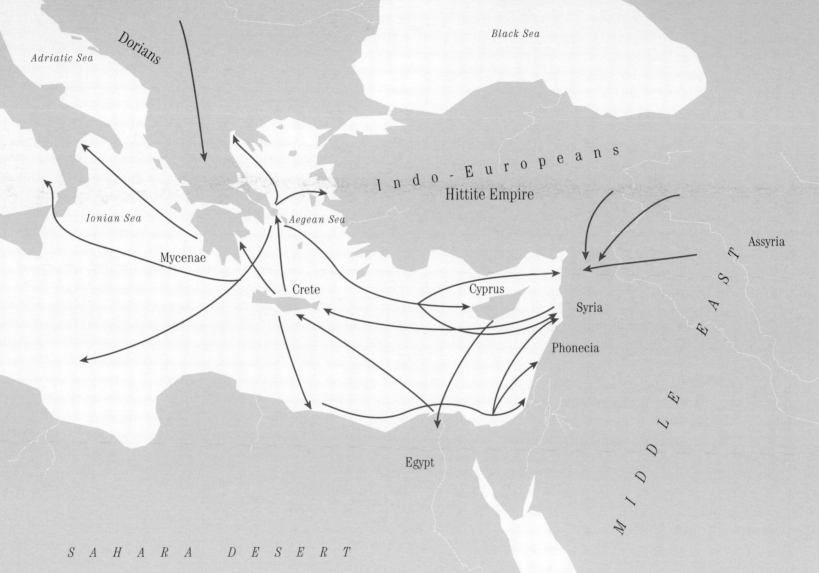

Caspian
Sea

Black Sea

Adriatic Sea

Dorians

Indo-Europeans

Hittite Empire

Ionian Sea

Aegean Sea

Assyria

Mycenae

Crete

Cyprus

Syria

Phonecia

M I D D L E   E A S T

Egypt

S A H A R A   D E S E R T

Kush Civilization

Red
Sea

novel ways—and all this well in advance of the rise of more characteristic Greek styles and institutions from about 800 BCE onward. Early Greeks traded extensively in Egypt and the Middle East, which is where key contacts took place. A number of centers benefited from these exchanges.

Crete: Minoan civilization. This distinctive civilization took shape about 2000 BCE on an Aegean island that was one of the main routes for Egyptian and Middle Eastern traders headed to Greece. Egyptian styles gained great influence, particularly in art; some scholars have even argued that Cretans were Egyptian immigrants. Even the animals depicted in art, like lions, had to be copied from Egyptian models, for they did not exist on the island. Cretan artifacts spread widely around the Mediterranean as the society gained in prosperity and perfected borrowed art forms.

Crete also blended Middle Eastern influences, even in its language. Cretans used Middle Eastern writing materials—the clay tablet. Their religion may also have contained strong Middle Eastern elements, with similar symbols, such as the bull and the dove. The combination, in sum, was highly syncretic, with Egypt providing components for art and science, the Middle East elements of religion and language. This dis-

tinctive fusion also affected the Greek mainland, where Cretan trade was active.

Cyprus. This island, farther east in the Mediterranean than Crete, was strongly influenced, particularly in pottery styles, by Crete. Contact with Assyria after 1450 BCE brought more Middle Eastern influence, but copper trade with Egypt increased at the same time. Again, Egypt's art held strong appeal. A Middle Eastern language (Phoenician) coexisted with Greek.

Mycenaean civilization. On mainland Greece, the level of culture and civilization was far inferior to that achieved in Egypt and the Middle East. In about 1500 BCE, Indo-European invasions created a new society around Mycenae, and after this contacts with Egypt, the Middle East, and Crete intensified. Contacts with Crete yielded many artisans as slaves, leading to a period of essential dominance by Cretan art. But local influences revived, producing a more genuine mixture. Mycenaean men thus wore full body costumes and let their beards grow, in marked contrast to Cretan styles.

Mycenaean Greece sent merchants and envoys to Egyptian and Middle Eastern cities, from which they imported significant influences. Egypt and the Middle East served as sources of technology, including chariots and

Mycenaean and Minoan Civilizations

▨ *Mycenaean civilization (approximately 1500 BCE)*

▨ *Minoan civilization (approximately 2000 BCE)*

■ *Mycenaean and Minoan civilizations*

Troy.

Aegean Sea

Iolcus.

ITHACA

Orchomenus

Thebes.

Athens.

Mycenae.
Tiryns.

Pylos.   .Sparta

MELOS

THERA

RHODES

Mediterranean Sea

Sea of Crete

Knossos.
Palaiokastro.
CRETE   .Zakro
Gournia.
Phaistos.

Evolution of Alphabets

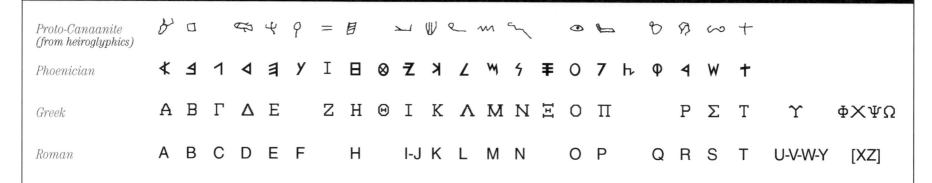

| Proto-Canaanite (from heiroglyphics) | | | | | | | | | | | | | | | | | | | | | | | | | |

spears, and architecture was a hybrid of Cretan, Egyptian, and local styles. Here was precedent for later borrowing, in post-Mycenaean Greece.

Renewed invasion, by the Dorians, ended the first exchange period by 1200 BCE, and civilization receded as new Indo-European influences gained ground—though the precise causes of Mycenaean decline remain unclear. By the ninth century, however, trade with the Middle East resumed, leading to additional religious imports, including common representations of gods and goddesses; new forms of magic were also brought in. A key import was the Phoenician alphabet, derived from Egyptian hieroglyphics and then modified into Greek. Artisans from both Egypt and the Middle East were attracted to or imported into this increasingly prosperous center, which in turn helped create for the first time the possibility of building large temples. Middle Eastern mercenary soldiers also brought in new forms of weaponry. Even the shields used by the famous Greek infantry were copies of devices introduced far earlier in the Middle East.

Greek civilization clearly owed much to contacts with predecessors. Borrowing emphasized precisely the items most commonly imitated from superior civilizations: writing, artistic styles, technology (including weaponry), and some religious elements. Less tangible features, like politics, loomed less large—at least according to available evidence. And Greece not only mixed its imports with local components, again a standard pattern, but also benefited by having an unusual number of influences that could be, and were, mixed with one another. Debate continues about how much was borrowed, but the result, in part because of imaginative combination, was no mere imitation. Greeks themselves respected the heritage of Middle Eastern and North African civilizations, but they downplayed borrowing and became rather disdainful of their contemporaries in these regions—another element that complicates the interpretation of contacts.

Suggested Readings

Martin Bernal, *Black Athena: The Afroasiatic Roots of Classical Civilization* (New Brunswick, N.J., 1987); Walter Burkert, *The Orientalizing Revolution: Near Eastern Influence on Greek Culture in the Early Archaic Age* (Cambridge, Mass., 1992); Arthur Cotterell, ed., *The Penguin Encyclopedia of Classical Civilizations* (London, 1993); Andrew Sherratt, *Economy and Society in Prehistoric Europe* (Princeton, N.J., 1997).

2. The Hellenistic-Indian Encounter

Toward the end of the fourth century BCE, armies from Macedonia, the kingdom north of Greece, swept through Greece and into the surrounding territories. They took advantage of division and decline in Greece but also recruited Greek officials and assimilated Greek culture; the great Macedonian conqueror Alexander the Great was tutored by the philosopher Aristotle. Alexander pushed conquests farther into Egypt (where Alexandria, a center of Greek learning, was founded) and through the Middle East, where he destroyed the Persian empire. Alexander, hoping to solidify his rule, encouraged a merger between Greek and Middle Eastern cultures. The result of the conquests and the cultural exchange is called Hellenism, suggesting predominant Greek influence but also significant departures from Greek principles. Hellenistic kingdoms lasted for about two centuries, with significant cultural legacies throughout the region that would be utilized by Roman, Byzantine, and Arab Muslim leaders. Alexander's approach, as well as the staggering scope of his conquests, was made to order for cultural exchange.

After defeating Persia, Alexander moved into India, setting up a more complex interaction with a significantly different cultural area. Some of the results of this interaction were dramatic but short-lived, suggesting the fragility of contacts between regions that had previously developed without direct mutual contact. Other results are debated, possibly significant but hard to trace. The exchange, between two of the great civilizations of the classical period, stands as a unique marker, suggesting the potential for more extensive contacts in the next world history period but also the limitations on mutual influence at a time when most energy was being devoted to constructing distinctive regional identities.

The Indian subcontinent had developed an elaborate culture between the great Indo-European migrations after 2000 BCE and the Hellenistic episode. Indian merchants—the most active in any civilization at the time—sailed to the Middle East and even traveled overland to the Mediterranean, but they felt little need to learn much about the culture there. Extensive contacts with

Alexander's Empire (323 BCE)

Alexander's empire

Alexander's march

Trade routes between India, the Middle East, and the eastern Mediterranean

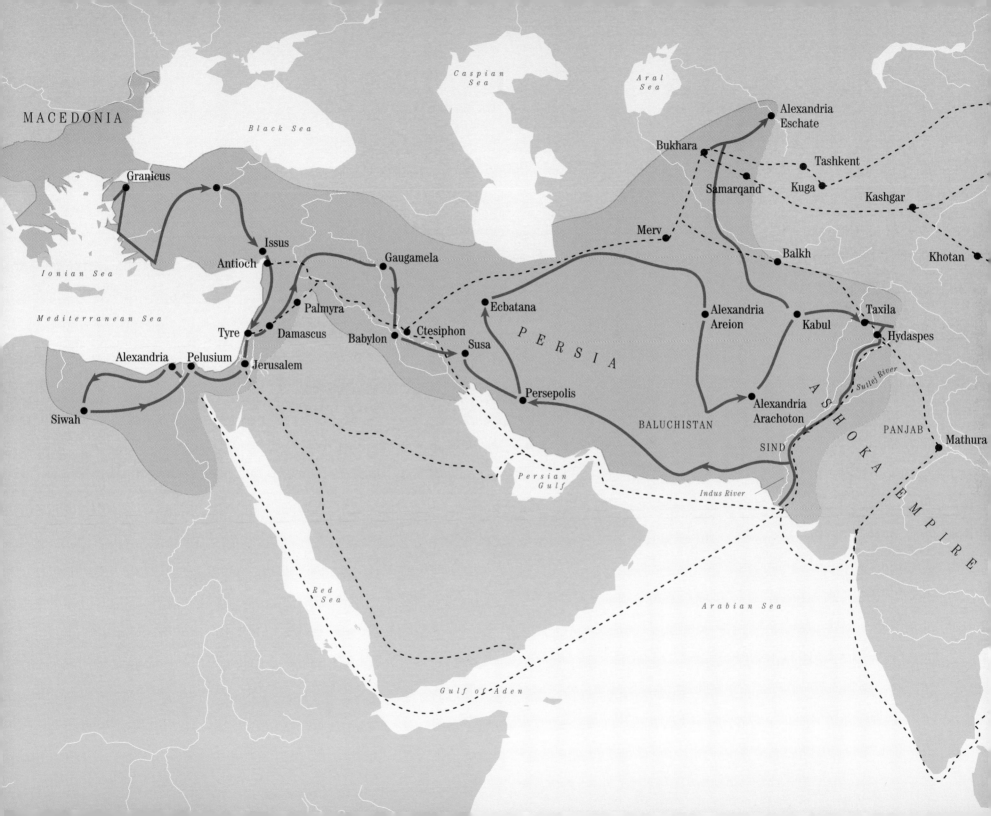

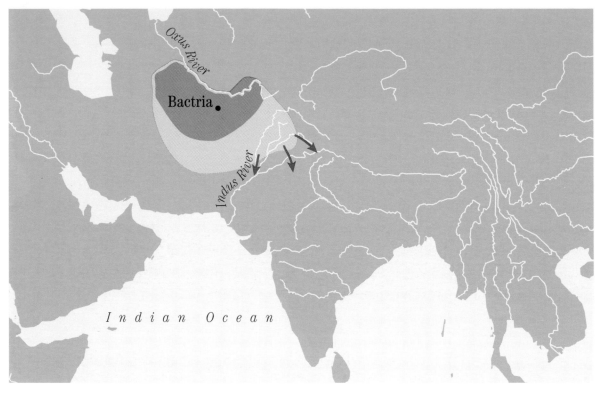

Bactrian Empire (300 BCE and 100 BCE)

 Bactrian borders
at 300 BCE

 Bactrian borders
after the Indian
campaign, 100 BCE

→ Bactrian raids
into India, 100 BCE

Persia were another story, and they did establish a pattern of imitation and interaction in northwestern India. In 327 BCE, India's peace was disturbed as Alexander the Great's army entered Panjab, India's northwestern province. For Alexander, the potential conquest of India would make him master of the world, for he knew little of China and was sure that his further victories would push him beyond any conqueror the world had known. He also was bored after a year of administering his new territories in the Middle East and wanted to keep his troops in fighting trim. Alexander's troops were outnumbered as they opposed the local Indian ruler, Porus, but as in previous campaigns they were better organized than their opposition. Confronting the war elephants that the Indians used caused some initial fright, but the Macedonian horsemen soon learned to cope. India itself was divided among rival princes, some of whom sided with the new conqueror, which facilitated progress.

Alexander pushed forward toward the Indus valley but was forced to stop at the Sutlej River in July of 326 BCE. His troops refused to cross the river and travel into India's heartland now that India's resistance was stiffening. Alexander acknowledged the inevitable and turned south into Baluchistan and the lower Indus (Western Sind) region, extending his rule to the shores of the Indian

Ocean by 325 BCE, when he left India and headed west for more campaigns. He divided his Indian territory into different regions and left Macedonian troops and rulers in charge. Several purely Greek-Macedonian cities were established in northwestern India and Afghanistan, filled with colonists and ringed by massive fortifications.

Alexander died of disease at Babylon in 323 BCE, throwing his empire into confusion. Quarrels broke out in Panjab and other Indian colonies among Macedonian rulers trying to seize more power for themselves. An Indian revolt in 317 BCE drove out many of the Macedonians, shrinking Hellenistic rule. The kingdom of Bactria remained, however, winning its independence from the rest of the Hellenistic Empire in 280. A series of Greek dynasties resulted, along with other, small Greek principalities. By the first century BCE, however, these Greek and partially Greek states had been destroyed, leaving no active trace. Trade between India and the Mediterranean persisted, into Roman times, maintaining some cultural contacts into the early centuries CE.

But Alexander's success had spurred Indians themselves to focus on more effective political and military systems. The ablest new ruler, Chandragupta Maurya (322–298 BCE), had helped push the Greeks back, then proceeded to found a considerable empire of his own. The Mauryan dynasty, later extended by the great emperor Ashoka (268–232 BCE), provided one of the leading empires in Indian history. This obviously put an end to further Greek penetration, though not to some additional mutual influence. Later developments in the Middle East itself drove new gaps between India and the Mediterranean. The rise of a new Persian (Sassanian) empire during the Roman period reduced contact, particularly cultural exchange, as did the rise of Islam during the seventh century CE. India and Mediterranean Europe would not encounter each other significantly again until the Portuguese voyages around Africa at the end of the fifteenth century.

Hellenistic-Indian contact was thus short-lived, as two otherwise separate civilizations, normally joined only by limited mutual trade, encountered each other seriously. What were the results, in terms of culture?

Hellenism in India

Alexander himself seems to have attempted little cultural contact with India—in contrast to his more active policies with Persia. Greek and Macedonian settlers did interact, however, though the Indians were hostile. Indians referred to the conquerors as "savage barbarians" and, as we have seen, pressed them to leave as quickly as possible. Many Greeks who remained converted to Hinduism or Buddhism and blended with the local populations.

Yet two categories of influence developed. First, Indian scientists were extremely interested in Greek achievements in astronomy and mathematics, and incorporated what they learned into their own scientific systems.

Second, briefly but dramatically, Indian artists utilized Hellenistic styles extensively. Greek-style figures were printed on Indian coins, as India learned the art of coinage from the Mediterranean. Greek monumental architecture influenced Indian designs, though the influence is harder to trace because the cities of the time have not survived. Art, including religious art, showed the most striking impact. The Buddhist school of art known as Gandhara formed in the first century BCE, using Hellenistic styles to portray Buddha and other religious scenes. The interplay was fascinating: Buddha, a thoroughly Indian figure, could be represented wearing Mediterranean-type togas, even hairstyles. Western travelers, not surprisingly, were impressed with the "superiority" of these changes in Indian styles. In fact, however, despite the surprising degree of imitation (or perhaps because of it), the movement trailed off rather quickly, leaving

no real, lasting trace in Indian culture. India did remain fairly open to outside influences, taking much from Persia and, later, from Islam. This brief exchange with a more remote civilization showed the potential power of contact, but also its constraints when not sustained by ongoing interaction.

Stone sculpture of Buddha (wearing toga)
Gandhara period
National Museum of Pakistan, Karachi
Borromeo/Art Resource

Suggested Readings

Arthur Cotterell, ed., *The Penguin Encyclopedia of Classical Civilizations* (London, 1993); Peter Green, ed., *Hellenistic History and Culture* (Berkeley, 1993); N. Ross Reat, *Buddhism: A History* (Berkeley, 1994); Jean Sedlar, *India and the Greek World* (Totowa, N.J., 1980); Vincent A. Smith, *The Early History of India from 600 B.C. to the Muhammadan Conquest* (Oxford, 1925); Erik Zurcher, *Buddhism: Its Origin and Spread in Words, Maps, and Pictures* (New York, 1962).

3. Buddhism and New Cultural Contacts in Asia

Buddhism, arising in the special religious context of classical India, generated some of the most striking cultural contacts in world history. Buddhism's dissemination began in the classical period but accelerated during the early centuries of the postclassical period, when its full geographical range was achieved. Becoming one of the three main world religions—and the one with the earliest origins—Buddhism shared features with Christianity and Islam, including devoted missionary activity and the prestige of accompanying political, commercial, and cultural features. Like its two counterparts, Buddhism clearly could straddle preexisting cultural boundaries, creating new contacts and exchanges in the process.

The spread of Buddhism also embraced a number of distinctive features, including the qualities of the religion itself. The religion proved unusually accommodating to local belief systems. As a result, the Buddhist zones of eastern, central, and southern Asia were only loosely linked in culture, as diverse forms of syncretism proliferated. The world of Buddhism was less united than

were the admittedly complex worlds of Islam and Christianity (though these religions, too, varied by region as they expanded). Buddhist contacts in different parts of Asia, as the religion moved out of India, were far more reciprocal than was the case with its religious counterparts.

Buddhism began as a reaction to specific features of India's priestly religion, Brahmanism—the religion that would evolve into Hinduism. In the sixth and fifth centuries BCE, as India turned into a fuller agricultural civilization, a host of religious reformers attacked the dominance of the Brahman priests and questioned the effectiveness of their religious rituals and sacrifices. Many proposed more personal meditation and discipline of the flesh while urging greater spiritual freedom for the masses. One reformer systematized these changes. Siddhartha Gautama (the Buddha), who lived from the mid-sixth century to the 480s BCE, was born into the warrior caste, where the hold of kings and priests was weak. Buddhist legend claims that the leader was the son of a local king whose religious powers had been

Spread of Buddhism in Asia

-------------- *Trade routes (including silk route)*

☐ *Cradle of Buddhism*

▨ *Spread of Buddhism until 6th century CE*

■ *Spread of Buddhism from 6th to 13th century CE*

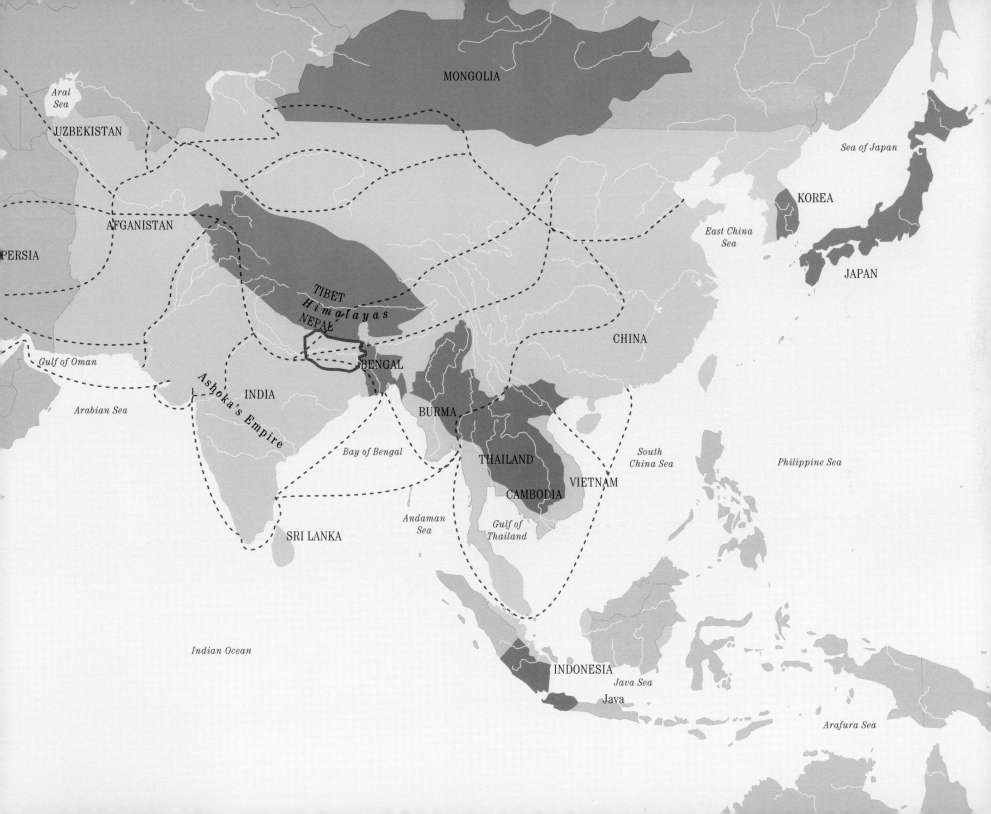

Aral Sea

UZBEKISTAN

PERSIA

AFGANISTAN

Gulf of Oman

Arabian Sea

Ashoka's Empire

INDIA

TIBET

Himalayas

NEPAL

BENGAL

Bay of Bengal

BURMA

THAILAND

CAMBODIA

VIETNAM

SRI LANKA

Andaman Sea

Gulf of Thailand

MONGOLIA

CHINA

Sea of Japan

KOREA

East China Sea

JAPAN

South China Sea

Philippine Sea

Indian Ocean

INDONESIA

Java Sea

Java

Arafura Sea

prophesied. As he became an adult, the Buddha wandered in the countryside, encountering human misery for the first time. He abandoned his claims on worldly power and imitated other Indian gurus, or religious leaders, by meditating in the wilderness and disciplining his body through yoga exercises and fasting.

The central problem for Buddhism was human suffering, for people begin to die at the moment of birth. Worldly pleasures are nothing but miseries in their own right, because they provide no durable satisfaction. Escape consists of abandoning all worldly desires, through meditation and enlightenment. Free from all attachments, the individual attains tranquillity, ultimately rising to nirvana, a union with the divine state. Buddha's travels and teachings won a considerable following, largely the poorer classes but also local rulers. His followers turned his teachings into an organized religion—against his own wishes. They accepted Hindu beliefs in reincarnation, disdain for any value on worldly goals, and hope for divine union. But they continued to attack priesthood and excessive ritual, and they also rejected India's unequal caste system, emphasizing the spiritual element in all people.

After Buddha's death, his followers spread his word and lived exemplary lives of holiness. They also claimed Buddha himself as a deity, though this was not part of Buddha's own teachings. Rival schools developed, each trying to compile authoritative written collections of the master's teachings and descriptions of his life. Popular Buddhism increasingly emphasized stories of the miracles Buddha performed, with graphic visions of heavenly pleasures and the tortures of a life without salvation. Buddhist monks retained the emphasis on meditation and renunciation of worldly pleasures, while ordinary people were urged to perform good deeds so as to merit spiritual advancement after death. Buddhist emphases particularly attracted lower Indian castes and women, regarded as capable of reaching nirvana. They, too, might participate in monastic life.

Buddhism also won the allegiance of the emperor Ashoka, who ruled the Mauryan empire between 268 and 232 BCE. Buddhism prompted Ashoka toward greater concern for the well-being of ordinary people. Ashoka also limited Brahman power and religious sacrifices. His efforts won hostility not only from the priests but also the warriors, but they converted many urban residents, including merchants, in a period of great Indian trade expansion. These merchants doubtless recognized the power of Buddhist spirituality, but it also welcomed a cultural alternative to the prestige of the traditional upper classes. Support from the emperor, who sponsored missionary efforts to Sri Lanka, to central Asia north of the Himalayas, and to the Middle East, and the active involvement of merchants capable of bringing religion to their ports of trade, backed by the credentials of their own commercial success, were crucial to the first Buddhist dissemination effort beyond the subcontinent of India. Early outposts in Sri Lanka provided a base for the spread of Buddhism to Burma, Java, and other parts of southeast Asia, while efforts in Nepal and central Asia provided ultimate contacts with Tibet and East Asia.

Ironically, Buddhism declined in India itself. Later rulers, particularly the Guptas (from the late third century CE onward), preferred Hinduism, seeking the support of priests and warriors. Indian Buddhism became increasingly concentrated in monasteries, leaving ordinary people more exposed to Hindu proselytizing. Some monasteries grew corrupt, benefiting from the support of wealthy patrons and removing themselves from the Indian people. Decline of international merchant activity, due in part to the growing disarray in China and Rome, reduced the importance of commercial adherents as traders became more dependent on the backing of local—Hindu—rulers. Buddhism's decline was gradual and mainly peaceful, as Hindus seldom persecuted Buddhists directly. But only small pockets of strength remained as the classical period ended.

Yet even as this occurred in the Buddhist homeland, the process of dissemination accelerated, prompting unexpected cultural contacts that provided new bases for this powerful spirituality.

Southeast Asia

Buddhism's movement outside of India involved a combination of deliberate missionary activity and the cultural impact of other facets of Indian influence, in politics and particularly in trade. India was the most active trading civilization in the classical world because of the relatively high status of its merchants and its favorable geographical location at a time when the Indian Ocean provided the most important trade arteries. Commercial outreach brought knowledge of Buddhism in its wake and created the aura of power and success that always facilitates adoption of new cultural systems.

The type of Buddhism that had particular impact on southeast Asia was the Theravada school, representing the "way of the elders." Buddhism in India split in the fourth century BCE, about a hundred years after Buddha's death, with the Theravada approach exemplifying the ideas closest to original Buddhist teachings. It emphasized the miseries of life in this world and the goal of personal salvation, through prayer and righteous practice, that takes one toward ultimate release in nirvana. This path depended heavily on individual effort; monks and other religious figures could illustrate the right way but had no obligation to save others.

Buddhism's first main extension occurred in Sri Lanka, an island that had long looked to India for examples of high culture and civilization. Ashoka sent the first missionaries, who reached Sri Lanka in about 250 BCE. As royal emissaries, they targeted the ruling classes, including the king, in the major cities, quickly winning many converts and soon spreading to other parts of the island. Within a century Buddhism became the area's dominant religion, bringing with it characteristic styles of art and architecture as well.

The Sri Lankan case formed something of a precedent for the spread of Theravada Buddhism in southern and southeastern Asia. The new religion mixed very little with local cultures, which, mainly polytheistic, offered little resistance in any event. Sri Lanka proved to be a vital breeding ground for missionary Buddhism, maintaining its active contacts with Buddhist groups in India but gradually becoming the world center of the Theravada school.

Buddhism's spread to southeast Asia, based on contacts both from India and from Sri Lanka, began in the third century BCE. Again Theravada missionaries took the lead, and again wider Indian influence created a favorable framework. Southeast Asia had strong trading ties with India, as most of the maritime trade routes were dominated by Indian ships. After the seventh century CE, Theravada Buddhism was rivaled by missionaries from China, from a different, Mahayana Buddhist school, and the two branches of Buddhism long coexisted in the region, particularly in Vietnam.

Renewed south Asian merchant activity in the twelfth and thirteenth centuries, spearheaded by traders from Sri Lanka, extended new trade routes and corresponding cultural influence and gave greater impetus to the Theravada approach. Burma, parts of present-day Indonesia particularly on the island of Java, and Thailand moved firmly to the Theravada camp, leaving only Vietnam, among southeast Asia's Buddhist territories, seriously divided. The region's substantial conversion to Buddhism again brought a growing impetus to Buddhist art and temple-building, adding another vital cultural ingredient to Southeast Asia. Kings in Burma, for example, competed with each other in temple-building. Royal backing helped maintain Buddhism despite invasions by outside groups, like the Mongols, whose conquests helped spread the religion to adjacent regions, like Cambodia.

Buddhism in Central and East Asia

Buddhism's spread to the north and east of India followed different patterns from those predominant in the southeast, in part because India had less-established trade contacts. This enhanced the need for cultural flexibility, as Buddhism had to interact with established cultures to gain a foothold. Further, the form of Buddhism that was most important in this set of cultural exchanges was not Theravada but Mahayana, or "Great Vehicle"—the second main branch of the Buddhist faith, which embraced a number of specific sects. Mahayana Buddhism deliberately went beyond tradition, and two distinctions gained emphasis. First, Mahayana groups combined interest in meditation and self-mortification with greater commitment to the acts of particularly holy leaders that might help gain salvation for the ordinarily religious. Rituals, including paying for religious verses, or sutras, could supplement prayer. Holy people, called bodhisattvas, or saints, sought particular purity not only for their own sake but to save other suffering mortals. Virtues included traditional Buddhist discipline, as well as wisdom, generosity, and service to others.

The second innovation of the Mahayana approach involved greater tolerance for prior cultural traditions, a more liberal outlook than Theravada stressed—and this was crucial not only to the penetration in the centralized, bureaucratic society of China but also to adaptations to beliefs in magic and sorcery in Mongolia and Tibet. The approach, clearly, allowed real flexibility in contact with diverse local traditions.

Buddhist entry into central Asia, along the Indian and Persian frontier and in present-day Afghanistan and Uzbekistan, involved both Buddhist strands. These were areas of significant Indian merchant activity, following the silk routes into these regions and on to the Middle East. Indian rulers also promoted Buddhism in hopes of establishing greater political unity, from the first century CE onward. Mahayana Buddhism flourished in the more northern regions, where traditional Indian influence was less dominant and where adaptations to the polytheism of local herding peoples were vital for Buddhist success. Theravada emphases did better in the south, in part because of support from rulers and townspeople accustomed to looking to India for example. In both cases, Buddhism's hold was fairly loose, particularly among nomadic tribes; the religion gripped the local elites primarily, though it flourished in these sectors until the fuller triumph of Islam by the eleventh century.

Buddhism came to Tibet late, in the seventh century, and it advanced only after the twelfth century, when it also spread to Mongolia. The process in Tibet was part of a more general and novel importation of Indian cultural influences. Missionaries brought in the religion, then combined it with beliefs in shamanism and supernatural forces. Mahayana approaches predominated as they merged with the indigenous religion, Bon. Missionary efforts for the stricter Theravada approach failed. Mahayana preachers realized the importance of ritual, given previous religious practices. Over time, however, the magical elements were combined with a more scholarly component. Mongol invasion of Tibet during the thirteenth century brought Tibetan Buddhism northward, where it encountered little cultural resistance.

Buddhism's spread to east Asia came from its niche in central Asia, as well as from the influence of Indian merchants trading in China. Traveling monks, missionaries, and silk traders brought the religion eastward from the first century onward. Again, adaptation was crucial, in this case to the political ideals of Confucianism. Buddhism took on such traditions as ancestor worship, and also emphasized the importance of family life. Buddhist spirituality won interest from the lower classes and the bureaucratic elite alike, from about the third century onward, as China suffered growing political and economic pressures and a wave of epidemic disease that greatly inflated the death rates. Buddhism's more otherworldly approach fit the moment, winning it many ardent converts and others who mixed Buddhist and Confucian or Daoist approaches for their own cultural amalgams. Ideals of personal salvation had obvious appeal amid growing political chaos, and many Buddhist missionaries added works of magic and miracles. Chinese Buddhism was not simply a top-down affair, as in Sri Lanka and central Asia.

Chinese Buddhism, cresting in the early stages of the T'ang dynasty in the seventh century, also penetrated Korea and Japan. Korea, where Buddhism entered in the fourth century, had long accepted powerful cultural influences from China. Upper-class converts, accordingly, played a leading role, vaunting Buddhism over local, indigenous religions. With royal support, Buddhism enjoyed great popularity between the seventh and fourteenth centuries, when it conveyed a special Korean identity to various social groups.

Buddhism entered Japan from China during the sixth century as part of a larger imitation process sponsored by the Japanese state—though it was resisted by leaders of the traditional Shinto faith. Buddhism became closely associated with the Japanese state, but popular appeal resulted from a syncretic merger with Shinto divinities, regarded as lesser aspects of Buddhist deities. Buddhist monks acted as caretakers for Shinto shrines and oversaw rituals. Buddhist doctrines and high art forms maintained elite interest, while works of practical healing and devotion appealed more to the lower classes.

The Buddhist Legacy

Lacking an organized church, divided into various sects, and, finally, merging with various local cultural influences, Buddhism both united and divided large parts of Asia. Buddhist monks could travel widely, but specific beliefs and practices varied greatly from one place to the next. This adaptability was a source of Buddhist strength, helping to explain its success in cultural contacts, but it also left the religion vulnerable to better-organized appeals or cultural counterattacks. Only pockets of Buddhism survived the Muslim surge in central Asia. Muslim success also restricted Buddhism in the Indonesian islands. China's ruling class turned against Buddhism in the ninth century, closing many monasteries and persecuting many faithful followers. Initial interest had turned to fear of Buddhism's lack of interest in the state and politics (despite official protestations of loyalty) and its otherworldly disdain for family values (including praise for celibacy). Buddhism survived in China, after centuries of serious religious and artistic influence, but it receded as a major force. Buddhism held on better in Korea, but Confucianism could rival its interest, as did missionary Christianity in the nineteenth century. New government backing for Confucianism in Japan, from the seventeenth century onward, limited Buddhism, as did later nationalistic revivals of Shintoism.

Buddhism remained a potent force. Asian migrations, to Hawaii and the Americas, for example, in the nineteenth and twentieth centuries, brought Buddhist minorities to new settings, where intense spirituality and flexible rituals and practices of personal discipline could win individual converts from the local populations. Buddhism remained a vital badge of cultural identity in Tibet, becoming a major bone of contention between this region and new Chinese communist rulers in the later twentieth century. Overall,

the Buddhist experience in world history offers one of the most significant, but also varied and distinctive, examples of cultural contact across immense geographical divides.

Suggested Readings

Jerry H. Bentley, *Old World Encounters: Cross-Cultural Exchanges and Contacts in Pre-Modern Times* (New York, 1993); N. Ross Reat, *Buddhism: A History* (Berkeley, 1994); Arthur Wright, *Buddhism in Chinese History* (Stanford, 1959); Erik Zurcher, *Buddhism: Its Origins and Spread in Words, Maps, and Pictures* (New York, 1962).

4. The Jewish Diaspora

The extensive migrations of Jews from their early base in what is now Israel form a distinctive chapter in the history of cultural contact. Millions of Jews have migrated over more than two thousand years, fanning out in the Middle East and North Africa, to a lesser degree in Asia and sub-Saharan Africa, extensively in many parts of Europe, and more recently in North America and other areas of European colonization. As they migrated, Jews often interacted with local cultures, providing new cultural elements and accepting new ones in turn—including language. But large numbers of Jews managed to preserve a coherent culture even as a sojourning minority, both when persecuted and when quietly welcomed. The result is a distinctive cultural achievement, still visible today, but also an important ingredient in the larger intellectual and artistic activities of a number of societies.

The origins of the Jews are shrouded in considerable mystery. A Semitic people, they migrated north from the southern Arabian peninsula. The first clear reference to Jews dates from about 1100 BCE, though Jewish religious stories place the people earlier, with enslavement in Egypt and then flight under Moses predating the definite historical record. A Jewish kingdom formed in the eleventh century BCE, and Jerusalem became its capital. By this time a distinctive religion was taking shape, durably emphasizing strict monotheism, with belief in Jehovah, for the first time in world history. Judaism also stressed ethical obligations and urged good treatment across social lines, though the inferiority of women was strongly stated, despite a central role in religious observances in the home. This religion provided the lasting basis of Jewish culture, but it emphasized the Jews themselves as a chosen people rather than encouraging missionary outreach. In this distinctive but particular religion lay the coherence of the Jewish experience over many centuries, but also the separateness emphasized by Jews and their neighbors alike. Jewish religious ideas began to be recorded in about 800 BCE, ultimately to be collected in the Torah, or the first five books of the Bible, and the Talmud.

Jewish Settlement in 300 CE

-------------- *Trade routes*

⟶ *Jewish dispersion routes*

▪ *Palestine, Jewish homeland*

▪ *Roman empire in 300 CE*

● • *Significant Jewish settlements*

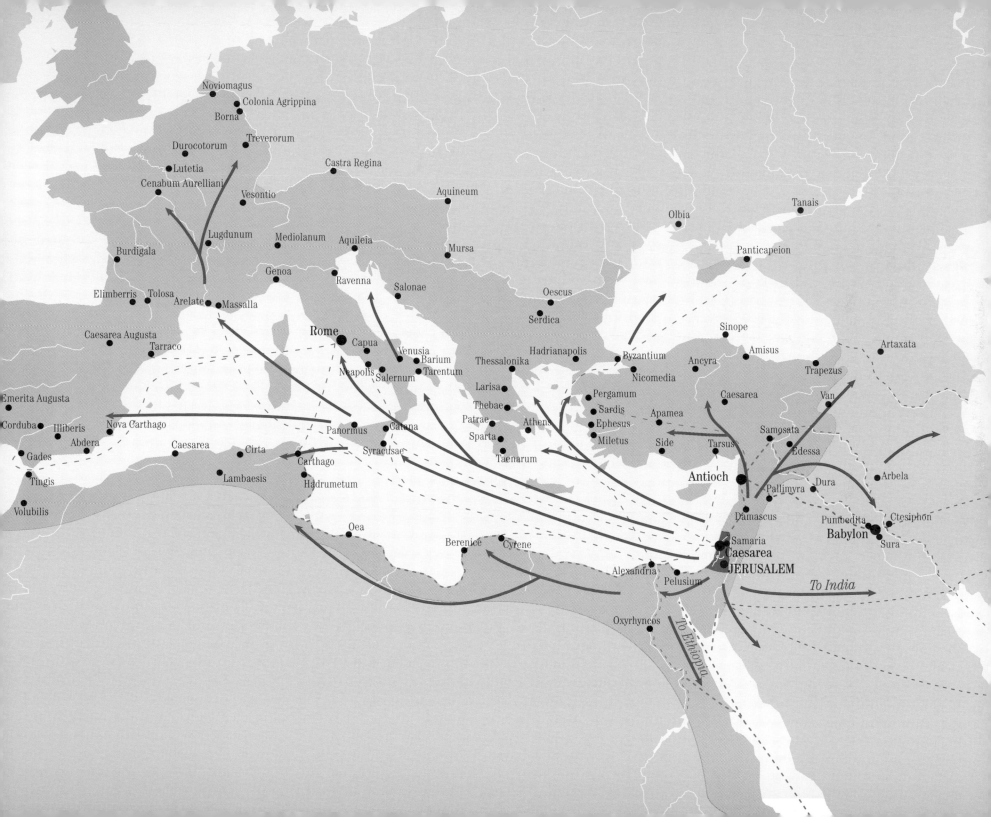

The Jewish political state did not last long. It was frequently overwhelmed by invaders of the Middle East. Babylonian conquest in the sixth century BCE saw many Jews taken prisoner and moved east, though they managed to preserve their religion. Some Jews remained in Babylonia. This was the first instance of the Jewish diaspora, the scattering of Jews outside what is now Israel. Under Hellenistic conquest, a number of Jews settled in Egypt, and through them use of the Greek language spread. By this point Jewish merchant activity had become considerable, helping to spread Judaism to areas like Ethiopia, where an important minority of African Jews, initially converts, existed until their movement to Israel quite recently. But Jews remained culturally isolated in the Hellenistic period; they considered Hellenism inferior and were themselves considered inferior in turn.

Rome conquered the Jewish homeland in 63 BCE. Suspicious of Judaism because it would not pay primary allegiance to the state, the Romans established unusually harsh military rule. A number of revolts occurred, but all ultimately failed. After a revolt in 132 CE, the Romans banned Jews from Jerusalem. This spurred the diaspora in earnest. Jews fanned out to many cities in the Middle East and North Africa, ultimately crossing to Spain. These Jews were ultimately known as Sephardic because they developed a syncretic style of art and costume in interaction with southern European, Arab, and other peoples; they also developed a distinctive language called Ladino. Another diaspora group spread through Roman holdings in Europe, moving into various Balkan regions, to France, and gradually farther north. This group, the Ashkenazi, mixed with various European peoples and ultimately developed a Germanic language called Yiddish. But both groups retained the Jewish religious faith, with only a few differences in ritual; both used Hebrew in religion; both felt themselves separate from neighboring populations; both developed a strong emphasis on commercial and urban activities.

In addition to these main Jewish groups, small but important clusters traveled as far east as India, where small communities still exist, having integrated with the caste system while preserving their Jewish religious identity.

Jews in the Middle East, North Africa, and Spain

Sephardic Jews interacted significantly with Muslims. Although Jews were regarded as religiously inferior by Muslims, and were sometimes persecuted, usually they were al-

Jewish dispersion routes

Sephardic cultural area (approximate)

Ashkenazi cultural area (approximate)

Significant Jewish settlements

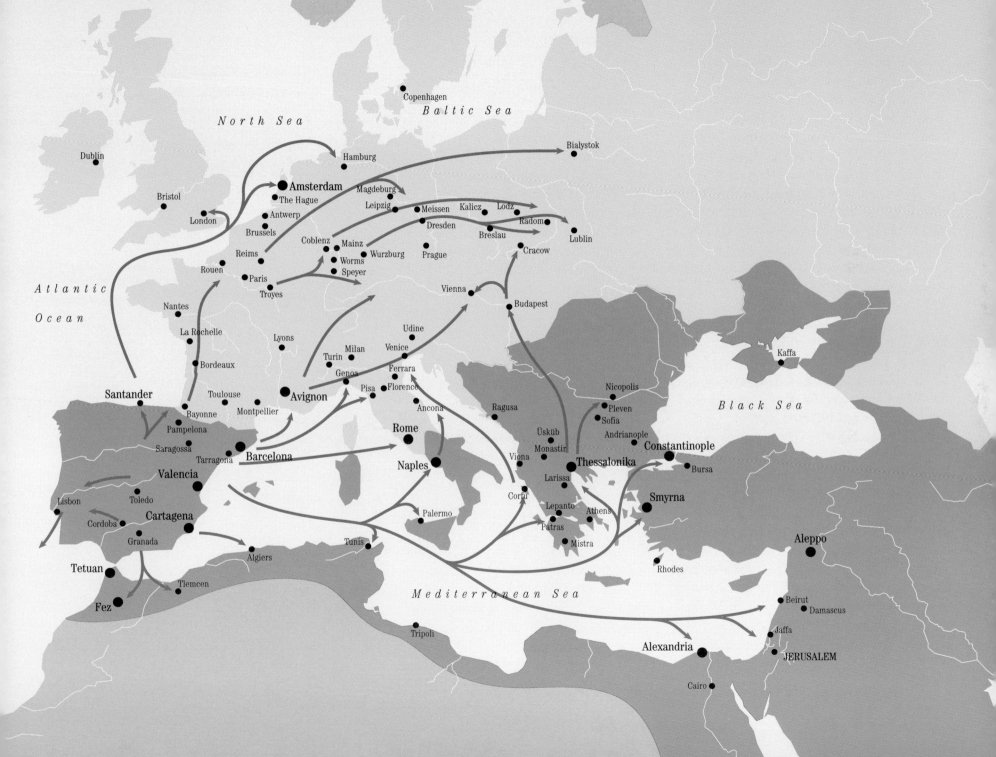

North Sea

Baltic Sea

Copenhagen

Bialystok

Hamburg

Dublin

Amsterdam

Magdeburg

The Hague

Bristol

Leipzig

Meissen

Kalicz

Lodz

London

Antwerp

Radom

Brussels

Dresden

Breslau

Lublin

Coblenz

Mainz

Atlantic

Reims

Worms

Wurzburg

Prague

Cracow

Rouen

Speyer

Ocean

Paris

Vienna

Nantes

Troyes

Budapest

La Rochelle

Lyons

Udine

Bordeaux

Milan

Venice

Kaffa

Turin

Santander

Toulouse

Genoa

Ferrara

Black Sea

Bayonne

Montpellier

Avignon

Pisa

Florence

Pampelona

Ancona

Nicopolis

Saragossa

Barcelona

Ragusa

Pleven

Tarragona

Rome

Sofia

Andrianople

Constantinople

Valencia

Üsküb

Monastir

Thessalonika

Bursa

Naples

Viona

Toledo

Larissa

Smyrna

Cartagena

Corfu

Lisbon

Palermo

Lepanto

Athens

Cordoba

Patras

Aleppo

Granada

Tunis

Mistra

Tetuan

Algiers

Rhodes

Tlemcen

Mediterranean Sea

Beirut

Fez

Damascus

Jaffa

Tripoli

Alexandria

JERUSALEM

Cairo

lowed a separate existence on condition of paying special taxes. Muslim leaders recognized a shared religious heritage while resenting Jewish reluctance to convert. Many Jews adopted Arabic as a second language, and Jewish scholars made significant contributions to Islamic science, philosophy, and medicine. Persian Jews were also famous for their music and dance, and many Jews served in the bureaucracy of the caliphate, where their loyalty seemed more secure than that of the Arab upper class precisely because they depended on political favor. Spain provided a fertile center for Jewish-Muslim cultural exchange between the tenth and the thirteenth centuries, with shared contributions in several sciences and in mathematics. This collaboration ended as Christians began to reconquer the peninsula. More generally in the Middle East, as Muslim culture deteriorated by the fourteenth century, the Jewish-Muslim link frayed somewhat. Jews began to regard themselves as culturally superior, and indeed they were more likely to be educated and literate. Muslim hostility to Jews gradually increased from the sixteenth century onward. Cultural interchange declined, partly because the two religions, both espousing a comprehensive way of life, were too similar to easily combine without loss of identity.

Jews in North Africa interacted strongly with Western colonial powers in the nineteenth and twentieth centuries, when British, French, and Italian governments took over the region. North African Jews became increasingly westernized, further separating them from their Muslim neighbors.

With the formation of the state of Israel in 1948, and as Israeli-Arab hostility grew, the Jewish minorities of North Africa and the Middle East encountered increasing persecution, with rare exceptions, as in Turkey. Many migrated to Israel, where they combined uneasily with the more powerful Ashkenazi immigrants.

The Diaspora in Europe and Beyond

Jewish migrants in Hellenistic and Roman Europe exchanged little with the dominant cultures. Romans regarded Jewish beliefs as inferior, as well as dangerous. Jews frequently learned Greek, and their Greek-language works—in literature, philosophy, and history—contributed importantly to Jewish intellectual life, but with little spillover to other Greek-speakers. For many centuries, Jewish and European Christian cultures seemed mutually exclusive. Many Christians resented Jews as the presumed killers of Christ and, more practically, for their commercial know-how and their willingness to

Location of World Jewish Population in 1998 (Approximately 13 Million)

- Million or more
- 100,000 or more
- More than 10,000, fewer than 100,000
- 1,000 to 10,000
- Fewer than 1,000
- → 20th century migration

risk lending money at interest. Kings borrowed from Jewish bankers and periodically expelled them as a means of avoiding repayment. Anti-Semitism became a deep-seated element of European culture. Many Jews were segregated within cities in ghettos. They were forbidden to own land or practice crafts, which logically increased their concentration on commerce and banking. Anti-Semitism in Western Europe increased as Christian fervor mounted during and after the Crusades, in the twelfth and thirteenth centuries, and most countries expelled Jews. Refugees settled in Poland, which soon boasted the largest concentration of Jews in the world, and a bit later in Russia. In spite of all of this movement many Jews preserved their cultural identity, including Yiddish language and art, as well as the Jewish religion itself.

Changes occurred from the seventeenth century onward as European Christianity divided and more secular ideas surfaced. Jews were by this point clearly participating in larger European cultural rhythms, sometimes unwittingly. For example, rabbis began to tone down often rowdy Jewish rituals, just as Christian leaders were trying to reduce popular spontaneity. Ceremonies like circumcision became much tamer, just as many Christian celebrations were muted. More formally, Jewish intellectuals like Mendelssohn in Germany and Spinoza in Holland began to question traditional religious beliefs and to urge greater emphasis on reason and science. This set the stage for extensive Jewish participation in the Enlightenment. At the same time, by the late eighteenth and early nineteenth centuries, many liberal reformers in Western and Central Europe began to repeal legal discriminations against the Jews. With a strong cultural emphasis on education and commerce, and now freed from legal disabilities, Jews began to play a disproportionate role in European intellectual and commercial life. Jews or people of Jewish origin, such as Karl Marx, Sigmund Freud, and Albert Einstein, surged to the forefront of cultural and political innovation. Jewish musicians, composers, and artists were also prominent. More generally, many Western European Jews, even when retaining their religion, began to take on Western habits, and reform movements within Judaism also sought to accommodate the religion itself to mainstream European beliefs. One symptom was the increasingly active role played by Jewish women, in religion and in political life, both in Europe and in North America.

These changes provoked a number of reactions. Some Jews worried about loss of identity and began to urge re-migration to the Jewish homeland in the Middle East. A trickle of these Zionist migrants began in the late nineteenth century. Anti-Semitism revived, and Jews were blamed for a host of modern ills. Further, in Eastern Europe, burgeoning Slavic nationalism often seized on Jews as scapegoats, attacking them in violent pogroms. These developments triggered important migrations; Central and Eastern European Jews moved to Western Europe, to centers in Latin America, to Canada and Australia, but above all to the United States, to which 3 million Jews would emigrate during the nineteenth and early twentieth centuries. American Jews became the largest Jewish population in the world by around 1900.

Nazi persecution of Jews before and during World War II, in which 6 million Jews were killed in the Holocaust throughout most of Europe, prompted the last great movement of European Jews. Some managed to flee to the Americas, joining established Jewish groups. Far more, after World War II ended, headed for Israel; more than a million Ashkenazi immigrants, joining established Zionists, effectively established the Israeli state and economy. The collapse of the Soviet Union in 1991, and the revival of persecution in Eastern Europe, drove another Jewish migration to the United States, Western Europe, and Israel.

The story of Jewish cultural interactions continued amid all these changes. Jewish "Westernization" persisted in many ways, despite the horrors of the Holocaust. The assimilation of many American Jews, including growing rates of intermarriage of Jews with non-Jews, raised concerns about the future of Jewish identity. Israel itself, eager to preserve religion and also to adapt Jewish culture to embrace more militant, aggressive values, encountered the power of international consumerism and media culture by the 1990s. But interaction remained a two-way street. American Jews contributed powerfully to the entertainment industry, as well as to academic life, and Jewish words and products such as *mensch* and the bagel became standard elements of American popular culture. Issues of Jewish identity and the contributions of Jews to larger international developments continue to shape world history in important ways.

Suggested Readings

Arnold Eisen, *Galut: Modern Jewish Reflections on Homelessness and Homecoming* (Bloomington, Ind., 1986); Raphael Patai, *Tents of Jacob: The Diaspora, Yesterday and Today* (Englewood Cliffs, N.J., 1971); Howard Sachar, *The Course of Modern Jewish History* (New York, 1990).

5. The Spread of Christianity

Like the Jewish diaspora, the spread of Christianity began in the classical period and has continued into recent times. This chapter deals with Christianity's spread in Afro-Eurasia, particularly in the classical and postclassical periods but with renewed development in the late nineteenth and twentieth centuries. Like Buddhism, and later Islam, Christianity developed into one of the great world religions, capable of transcending a host of geographical and cultural boundaries because of the power of its appeal. Like the other world religions, however, Christianity's spread led to a number of compromises with local belief systems, in various patterns of syncretism that involved complex mixtures of religious change and continuities. These patterns, along with explicit doctrinal disputes, helped divide Christians into separate and sometimes hostile communities.

Christianity originated in the eastern Mediterranean during the reign of the Roman emperor Augustus, initially as a reform movement within the Jewish religion. Just as Buddhists protested excessive Hindu cer-emonialism, so Jesus of Nazareth argued against the rigidities that had arisen in the Jewish priesthood. The new religion also appealed to some of the poorer classes, with promises of opportunities of salvation and the imminence of the kingdom of God on earth. Jesus seems to have seen himself as a Jewish prophet and teacher who probably came to believe that he was the son of God. (Certainly his followers came to believe this of him—we lack direct evidence of his own beliefs.) Jesus urged a moral code based on love, charity, and humility. Many of his disciples believed that a Final Judgment was near at hand, and through it God would reward the righteous with immortality and condemn sinners to everlasting hell. Opposition from Jewish leaders and the Roman governor led to Jesus's crucifixion in about 30 CE. Belief that Jesus Christ was resurrected seemed to confirm his divinity, and his followers began to spread his word around the eastern Mediterranean. When one early convert, Stephen, was stoned to death, many disciples left Israel and traveled throughout western Asia. The gradual realization that the Messiah was not imme-

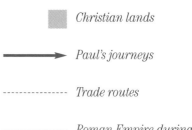

Spread of Christianity through the 6th Century CE

Christian lands

Paul's journeys

Trade routes

Roman Empire during rule of Constantine (4th century CE)

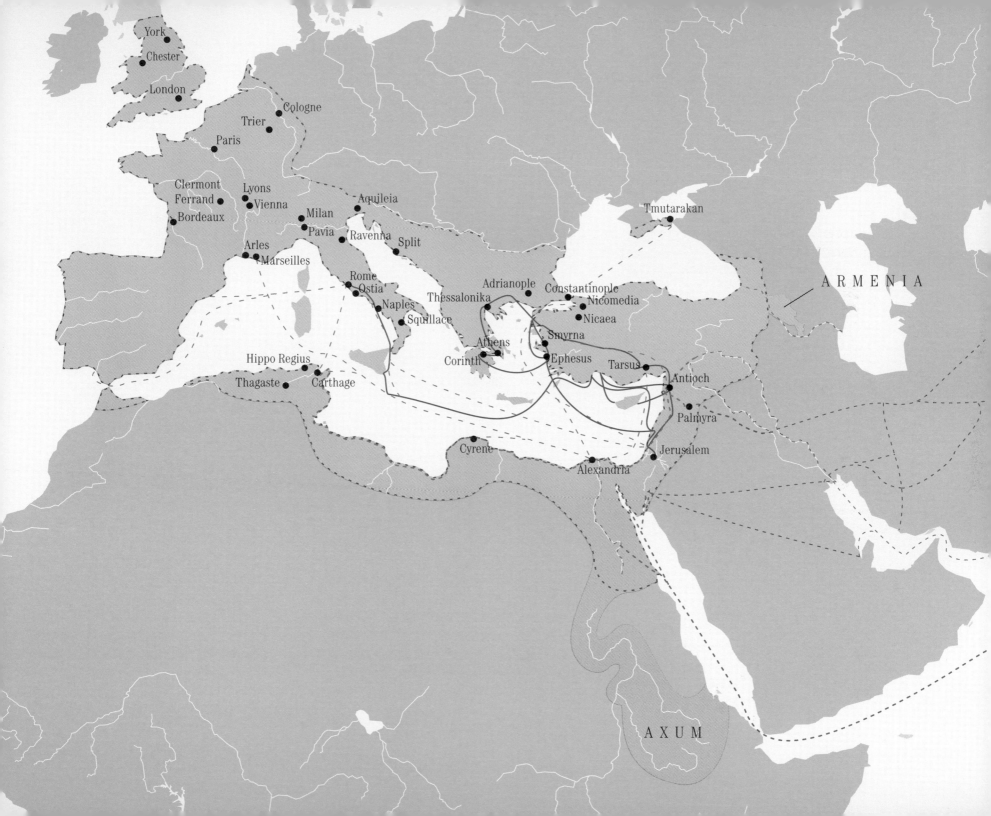

diately returning to earth to set up God's kingdom also contributed to growing efforts to spread and institutionalize the religion.

A crucial step toward Christian missionary activity came under the apostle Paul, a Jewish convert (about 35 CE) who argued that this religion was not for Jews alone. Rather, in the spirit of the more cosmopolitan Roman Empire and Middle Eastern Hellenism, Paul's leadership established that Christianity was universal and available to all, whether or not they followed Jewish law. Paul himself preached widely, in Greece and Italy as well as the Middle East, and he increasingly phrased the religion in terms of Greco-Roman culture (and using the Greek language), creating a more formal theology that appealed to those outside the poorest groups.

Christianity spread gradually throughout the Roman Empire, taking advantage of the ease of travel that political unity provided. Roman governments occasionally attacked the new religion, which refused to place loyalty to the emperor above God, but they were often tolerant; sporadic persecution did produce martyrdom, which had its own powerful impact on the spread of Christianity. Gradually church officials emerged, as did a more formal body of intellectual work. By the fourth century, Christian intellectuals had become one of the most creative forces

in the empire; about 10 percent of the population had converted, finding in this religion a spiritual focus and rituals that mainstream Roman religion, with its secular-seeming gods and goddesses, did not provide. It was in the fourth century that the emperor Constantine made Christianity the official religion, which greatly accelerated conversions in southern Europe (Spain and Italy), parts of the Balkans, and particularly in the eastern Mediterranean and North Africa.

Even before this, Christianity had been adopted by the ruler of Armenia, a Roman province in Western Asia and the first region to make Christianity an official religion. Traders and missionaries also spread Christianity beyond Rome's borders in the Middle East (to Persia, for example), though the religion was regarded with suspicion by the priests of Persia's Zoroastrian religion and the rulers of the Sassanid empire there, hostile to all things Roman.

Christianity also spread in this early period to Axum, in northeastern Africa below Egypt. Here, active trade with the Middle East and Greece encouraged cultural contact, and Christianity seemed part of a vibrant, successful society. King Ezana made this the official religion. Christianity in this part of Africa, particularly Ethiopia, was cut off by Muslim conquest of North Africa in the seventh century. A separate Ethiopian

church persisted, resuming some contact with European Christians in the thirteenth century; today about 40 percent of Ethiopians are Christian.

Christianity's spread, in the final period of the Roman empire, was complicated by various doctrinal disputes. Egyptian Christians (known as Coptics) emphasized, for example, the unity of Christ's human and divine nature. But the dominant religious leadership of the empire, in the Council of Chalcedon (451 CE), ruled that Christ had two separate natures. Most Egyptian faithful refused to accede, and a separate Coptic church persists to this day, with about 3 million adherents, mainly in Egypt. Muslim invasion led to many Christian conversions throughout North Africa, reducing the Coptic presence in the region.

After the collapse of the full Roman Empire in the fifth century, the most successful missionary efforts looked northward, to Europe. The Western church, under the pope in Rome, sponsored a host of missionary campaigns, gradually converting most of the Germanic peoples from their traditional polytheistic religions. A Frankish king, Clovis, adopted the religion in 496 CE. Missionaries soon thereafter spread Christianity to the British isles (the pope sent a group of forty missionaries at the end of the sixth century, and their efforts gradually superseded those of earlier Celtic leaders, whose Christianity had initially developed more separately). Later still the religion reached northern Germany and, by the tenth century, Scandinavia. Conversion of these regions brought not only religion but also the Latin writing system and larger artistic and intellectual apparatus associated with Roman Christianity. Other Catholic missionary efforts reached into central Europe, converting the Czech areas, Hungary, and Poland.

A largely separate dissemination effort came from the Byzantine Empire, based in Constantinople. Eastern Orthodox Christianity differed with Catholicism on a number of doctrinal and organizational points; among other things, Eastern Orthodox Christians refused to accept the primacy of the pope in Rome. A full schism occurred in 1054 CE. Orthodox missionaries gradually converted peoples in the Balkans. In 854 CE the Byzantine government sent the missionaries Cyril and Methodius farther north, to places like present-day Slovakia, where they devised what would be called Cyrillic, a written script for Slavic languages derived from Greek letters. Here too, the spread of religion was associated with writing and other important linkages with a sophisticated artistic and literary culture. Trade advantages also played a part. A king in Kievan Russia, Vladimir I (ruled 980–1015 CE), adopted orthodox Christianity and forced

his subjects to convert by applying military pressure and by importing priests from Byzantium.

The spread of Christianity in virtually all parts of Europe was associated with important syncretic compromises with local beliefs. Christianity was monotheistic, but growing worship of local holy figures, or saints, restored some of the more traditional qualities of religion, in which a larger number of spiritual forces are available for support, some with strong local connections. Saints also served as mediators between ordinary people and a powerful God. Christians adopted polytheistic holidays; Christ's birth came to be celebrated not when it had occurred (almost certainly in the spring) but in association with the old rituals of the winter solstice. Other beliefs and practices, some of which appear magical or superstitious, adapted local folk traditions to Christian ideas. In Western Europe, a full campaign against what came to be known as popular superstition was mounted only in the sixteenth to seventeenth centuries.

Christianity in Asia

Christianity retained a strong hold in western Asia, though Muslim conquests cut into its ranks. Important Christian minorities persisted in places like present-day Lebanon,

usually tolerated by Muslim authorities on condition that Christians paid a higher tax. Byzantine Christians in Asia suffered as the territory of the empire shrank, and then encountered still greater pressure after Turkish conquests in the fifteenth century. Armenian Christians also suffered at various points in the Ottoman period, though the church (part of Eastern Orthodoxy) retained a substantial following.

Outside the old boundaries of the Roman Empire in Asia, much early Christian activity was conducted by neither of the main European churches, but by a group called Nestorians. (Another movement, the Manicheans, who originated in Persia, also used Christian elements along with elements of Zoroastrianism and even Buddhism, and won considerable missionary success in Central Asia and beyond, setting up a community even in China that lasted until government persecution wiped it out in the sixteenth century.)

Nestorius was a patriarch in Constantinople who argued that divine and human natures coexisted in Christ. The patriarch's beliefs, and his personal arrogance, roused opponents, who argued that this approach overdid the human elements in Christ's nature. The Roman pope excommunicated Nestorius in 430 CE. But his ideas survived in Mesopotamia and Persia, where opposition to Rome actually helped them catch on. Islamic conquerors of the region allowed Nestorians to keep their faith, though most converted to Islam in part because of special taxation. Already, however, Nestorian merchants had spread the ideas into India, central Asia, and China. They won no support from established rulers—a crucial difference from Europe. But they displayed a bit of the flexibility, the willingness for syncretism, characteristic of most successful missionary efforts, so they did win some followers. A Tang emperor was interested in Nestorian ideas (brought by a Persian bishop), which he found somewhat similar to Buddhism, and a monastery was allowed in the city of Changan in the seventh century despite Buddhist and Daoist opposition. Chinese Nestorians used Buddhist and Daoist vocabulary, writing verses called the "Jesusi-Messia Sutra," for example, and calling angels and saints "buddhas." But Christianity seemed alien to most East Asians, and government persecution also inhibited conversions.

The final Nestorian chapter came in the Mongol period. Mongol leaders in Persia, converted to Islam, turned furiously against the Nestorians in the early fourteenth century. Muslim crowds destroyed churches, looted homes, and killed or enslaved many individuals. Nestorianism was wiped out in western Asia. Mongol leaders in China, how-

ever, were broadly tolerant, actively interested in many religions, and they used Nestorian officials and secretaries, among others, though they rarely found Christianity attractive personally. European Catholics, visiting China, attacked Nestorians for holding "false beliefs," but they made little missionary headway of their own (mainly serving Western merchants, until trade fell off after the collapse of the Mongol empire). With the decline of the Mongols, indeed, the Nestorian minority in central and eastern Asia was diminished further, attacked by Confucian and Muslim governments, even as Nestorians themselves proved unwilling to compromise basic doctrines and rituals that continued to seem foreign.

As Western European trade expanded by the sixteenth century, Catholics sent new missions, by sea, to India and China. The missionaries won some converts, particularly in India, but their success roused the active resistance of local religious leaders. Many missionaries adopted local dress and manners. The famous Jesuit Matteo Ricci, in China, won tolerance because of his scientific knowledge and his ability to construct superior clocks. He wore Confucian dress and adopted Confucian manners, mastering the language and the literary classics. But he and his colleagues won little religious interest. A Jesuit leader in India adopted Brahmin habits, including vegetarianism, but he

Spread of Christianity 500–1000 CE

■ Catholic area

■ Coptic area

■ Orthodox area

■ Nestorian area

– – – ▶ Catholic, Coptic, and Orthodox missionary routes

– – – ▶ Nestorian missionary routes

Kiev

Rome

Chalcedon

Constantinople

MANICHEANS

To China

Changan

too made little headway and was denounced by other missionaries as having converted to Hinduism. Christians won more converts in Japan, but the government turned against them in the late sixteenth century. Only in the Philippines was substantial headway made; except for Islam in the south, no world religion or major philosophy had a prior hold. Asians in the main saw no reason to switch their beliefs. Among Europeans, Protestants at this point had little missionary interest in any event, and the great merchant companies from Protestant regions concentrated on gaining trade advantages through the eighteenth century.

Christianity's most recent Asian (and African) chapter involved the huge burst of missionary activity, both Catholic and Protestant, that spread from the mid-nineteenth century, fueled by imperialist success, industrial prosperity, and a desire to "civilize" the whole world in the Western image. Missionaries still made little headway in Asia, save in Korea, where a large minority became Christian. But missionaries there converted a number of individuals and set up schools, and this played a role in important movements of reform, including efforts to improve conditions for women (many leaders of initial attempts to ban footbinding in China, for example, were converted Christians backed by European and American missionaries).

The story was different in Africa. European coastal settlements had generated limited conversions before the modern missionary era. Backed by colonial governments and growing trade penetration, however, large numbers of African polytheists converted from the late nineteenth century onward. By the late twentieth century, about 40 percent of all sub-Saharan Africans were Christians (evenly divided, Protestant and Catholic). Christianity seemed to many Africans a key to success in Western terms (including jobs in colonial administrations). It appealed to groups held as inferior under traditional cultures, including many women. And it offered undeniable spiritual appeal in a period of rapid and varied cultural change in the huge subcontinent.

Suggested Readings

Jerry H. Bentley, *Old World Encounters* (New York, 1993); Kenneth S. Latourette, *A History of Christianity* (New York, 1953); R. A. Markus, *Christianity in the Roman World* (New York, 1974).

Part II
Postclassical and Early Modern Periods, 450–1750 CE

The great classical empires fell or readjusted between 200 and 500 CE. Unity in the Mediterranean was shattered permanently with the collapse of Rome; China went through a long period of political disorder; India returned to more regional political patterns with the end of the Gupta empire. These developments set the stage for a new wave of cultural contacts. Precisely because political arrangements began to misfire, people were open to new belief systems, particularly through religion, that would provide different kinds of assurances. Revision of political boundaries also opened the way for new travels by merchants, missionaries, and migrant peoples.

The postclassical period (450–1450) saw the establishment of much more regular trading contact between Asia, Africa, and Europe. The principal routes ran east–west, from China and southeast Asia to the Middle East and East Africa, and from the Middle East to Europe. But subsidiary routes connected sub-Saharan Africa with the Middle East, both northwestern and northeastern Europe with the Middle East and Africa, and Japan with China. This intricate network obviously accelerated cultural exchange. The new religion of Islam was most elaborately involved in this process, as both a cause and a consequence of expanded patterns of contact, but there were other results as well.

The spread of world religions, launched earlier, accelerated, establishing much of the new framework for world history in the postclassical centuries. Chapters 3 and 5 outlined ongoing contacts resulting from Christianity and Buddhism. The development of Islam, beginning in about 600 CE, added a tremendous spur to cultural outreach, as this religion outpaced all others for several centuries.

Beginning in the fifteenth century, in what is usually called the early modern period of world history, Western Europe began to gain new prominence in world trade, thanks to aggressive ambitions and the advantages provided by Europe's lead in the manufacture of gunnery. A key development involved the inclusion of the Americas in international cultural contacts for the first time, and then the island areas of the Pacific, as European missionaries pressed the spread of Christianity to these additional areas. Changes in West European culture, featuring the rise of science, provided a much newer kind of impetus for contact.

Scientific ideas had spread before; the West, for example, had learned from Arab and Jewish scientists. But science had never been so prominent in intellectual life as it now became in Western Europe, or carried such potential for promoting technological and economic advances. The effort to copy Western science, then, added a vital new dimension to international cultural history. Precisely because such substantial adjustments were involved, the effort was geographically uneven: some societies proved readier to import this new component than others.

Finally, Europe's surge in world trade and its effort to exploit its new holdings in the Americas created a major, forced movement of people, in this case enslaved Africans. The resultant African diaspora led to complex cultural combinations, as transplanted Africans adjusted to new languages, styles, and beliefs while also retaining important core traditions and influencing the cultures around them in their new homes.

6. The Spread of Islam

One of the great cultural contact experiences in world history involved the spread of Islam, from its initial base in the Arabian peninsula and the Middle East to a host of areas in Africa, Asia, and Europe. Islam appealed to people in a variety of societies and cultures, bringing important changes as a result of contact while often in some respects merging with the established local belief systems.

Muslims compelled new cultural contacts from about 700 CE onward as a result of conquests, far-reaching trade, and, increasingly, missionary activity. The geographical dimensions of the Muslim world were pretty well established by 1450 CE—the end of the postclassical period—though a few key later chapters would be written in Africa, southern Asia, and southeastern Europe. Islam's spread was gradual though amazingly rapid given the extensive geography and diverse regions involved.

Two primary patterns were involved. In some cases, Islam spread to other cultures in a context of military conquest, even though the religion was tolerant of other beliefs. Muslims rarely forced people to convert to their religion, often preferring to levy a special tax on minority communities instead. The famous jihad, or holy war described by the prophet Muhammad, was mainly used for defense of the faith, not forced conversion, though there were exceptions. But the success of Muslim armies could create a context in which other people found it prudent to convert, or in which they were attracted to the religion simply because of its manifest power and triumph. In other instances, Islam spread through more spontaneous conversions as people learned of it through trade and missionary activity. The religion was clearly attractive, with an explicit set of beliefs about what to do and what not to do in order to win access to heaven and avoid a lamentable eternity in hell. It appealed to lower-class groups because of its commitment to charity and spiritual equality; it also legitimated merchant activity more than did most belief systems at the time, and so could attract traders. The

Extent of the Islamic World by 1500 CE

■ Lands conquered by Islamic military force

■ Lands where Islam was spread by Sufi missionaries and traders

→ Trade routes

Norwegian Sea

North Sea

*Moscow   *Kazan   *Ufa

Kiev.

Antwerp   *Azov   *Astrakhan   *Aral*
                                                                    Sea
Genoa   Venice.   Black Sea   Baku.   T R A N S O X A N I A   Tashkent   Kucha
Marseilles   Istanbul   Trebizond   *Caspian*   Bukhara   Samarqand   Kashgar   Suchou   *Kanchou   Peking
                                  B Y Z A N T I N E   E M P I R E   Tabriz   *Sea*   Merv   Balkh   Khotan   Lanchou
Lisbon   Tunis   Hangchou
Tangier Ceuta   Algiers   Barqa   Damascus   Baghdad   *Isfahan   Herat   Kabul   Fuchou
Rabat Fez   Tripoli   P E R S I A   Lahore   Yunnan-fu
Marrakech   Alexandria   Cairo   Damascus   Basra   Shiraz   Delhi   Canton
Agadir   Mecca.   Hormuz   D E L H I   S U L T A N A T E
                                                                                        Muscat   Cambay   Chittagong
Awdaghost   Bay of Bengal   South
Walata Timbuktu   China Sea
GHANA   Gao
A   Kukawa   Al Fasher   Sennar   Calicut   Timor Sea
M   Katsina Kano   Harar   Zaila
    Zaria   Massina
                                                                                        Mogadishu
                                                                              Lamu.   Indian Ocean
                                                                        Mombasa.
                                                                        Zanzibar
                                                                    Kilwa

cultural and political achievements of Islam drew people eager to advance their societies in a variety of ways, including religious ones.

Believing that he was divinely inspired, the prophet Muhammad, born in about 570 CE, generated the basic tenets of the newest world religion. The context for Islam involved the surge of Arab peoples, originally a nomadic group on the fringes of Mediterranean civilization that became increasingly active in trade and formulated a well-established culture, including a writing system. The collapse of the Roman Empire had left a welter of small states in the eastern Mediterranean, along with a confusing mixture of religions, including Judaism and Christianity. Muhammad sought to reorganize Arab culture but also to offer a religion that would build on and perfect Jewish and Christian thinking. Islam was a rigorous monotheistic system, offering a clear statement of duties that would help assure salvation. The Qu'ran, the holy book that Muhammad composed under the inspiration of Allah, provided detailed regulations for many aspects of life, including family life. Muslim principles urged rulers to defend the religion above all, though their political goals were often unfulfilled; Islam came to depend on a mixture of state support and the activities of scholars and legal philosophers who interpreted doctrine and law on a local basis and administered a system of religious courts.

Islam had begun to spread rapidly among the Arabs by the time of Muhammad's death in 632 CE. This growth helped galvanize Arabs to a surge of conquest, and armies quickly spread through the Middle East, including Persia, though the Byzantine Empire long held out amid reduced Asian territory. North Africa was another early conquest. A loose central government, the caliphate, was established for this West Asian–North African heartland by Muhammad's successors; it lasted until the thirteenth century. Arabs for a time sought to reserve Islam for their people alone, while tolerating local religions; but many people in the conquered regions sought access, some of them adopting Arab language and culture in the process. Conquests by Muslim Arabs gradually turned into a more general spread of Islam in its Middle Eastern–North African heartland and beyond.

The Middle East had long been a center of trade with Asia, Africa, and Europe alike. Arab and Muslim gains spurred further efforts toward achieving additional wealth, which were aided by Islam's approval of merchant activity leavened by charity. Muslim traders spread well beyond the caliphate, and they left new cultural contacts in their wake.

Finally, changes in Islam itself galvanized even more active and extensive spiritual leadership. After about 900 CE a movement called Sufism took hold. The movement emerged gradually and was fully defined only in about 1200 CE. Sufi leaders worried about the luxury and secular interests of the later caliphs, and also the diverse intellectual life that had developed as Islam interacted with Greek scientific heritage and various literary movements. They wanted a stricter focus on religion and a more intense piety. Interestingly, Sufi leaders, who initially flourished among outlying peoples like the Turks, borrowed some ideas from the Christian monastic movement and from Buddhism. Some Sufi leaders emphasized works of charity, but others offered a highly emotional religion complete with intense rituals. Characteristically, Sufi leaders sought to spread the beliefs of Islam to new regions. Their enthusiasm and the example of their holy devotion helped to persuade many people, as they showed how to bridge the gap between Allah and ordinary mortals.

From its base in the Middle East–North Africa, Islam gained adherents in several parts of southern Europe; in sub-Saharan Africa; in central Asia, including western China; in India; and in southeast Asia. The dates and patterns of growth varied in each case. In explaining how Islam caught on, a crucial variable involves the balance between conquest versus trade and spiritual example. Another division, when Islam spread mainly by persuasion, involves relationships between elites and masses of the receiving areas. In some cases elites and ruling classes converted first, attracted by the religion but also by its praise for merchants and its political success; elites then disseminated the religion further. In other cases, conversion began among ordinary people, as when Sufi leaders interacted with peasant villages.

Inevitably, as Islam surged into areas of different traditional beliefs and styles, cultural amalgamations occurred. Some areas received the religion fully, including its associated artistic styles, such as the architecture of the mosques and the rich decoration of a religion that tried to forbid representations of people and animals. Other areas, however, accepted the religion but not some of the specifics concerning art or family life. A variety of patterns of syncretism, or cultural blending, occurred. Finally, some areas saw the development of an important Muslim minority along with resistance by the majority culture. Tracing the geography of Islam means exploring these various and important results.

Islam and Europe

The rise of Islam created fear and hatred in Christian Europe, which quickly identified a powerful and indeed long superior rival. European crusades, called in the late eleventh century, sought to win back the Holy Land from the Muslims, though they were only briefly successful. Hostility to Islam has remained a major theme in European history to the present day. For their part, Muslims often scorned European backwardness and crudeness, and when Europe became more powerful, they often pointedly avoided opportunities for imitation and interaction.

But significant contacts occurred. Muslims made two separate sweeps into Europe, the first of which created an important cultural fusion, vital to European and even American history later on, and the second of which created a durable pocket of Muslims still active today.

The Arab conquests in Spain followed from their rapid sweep through North Africa in the seventh century. Conquests of Spain were complete, save for a Christian remnant in the northeast, by 732 CE. Frankish armies defeated the Muslims in France, blocking further gains; and a brief hold over Sicily and other Italian islands was pushed back by Christian invaders. But the Muslim period in Spain and Portugal had vital consequences. Muslim rulers developed an elaborate political and cultural framework while largely tolerating Christian subjects. A number of Spaniards converted under the influence of conquest and Muslim success. Muslim artistic styles long influenced Spanish architecture and decoration, even after Islam itself had been pushed out. Music, including the guitar, an Arab instrument, merged traditions as well—and from Spain the new styles would later spread to the Americas. Centers of learning, like Toledo, drew scholars from all over Europe, eager to take advantage of Muslim and Jewish science and philosophy; the result helped spur change and development in European intellectual life.

Amid all this fruitful interaction, Christian warriors from northern Spain mounted a steady counterattack, gradually winning back territory from the tenth century onward. The strength of Christianity and, ironically, limited trade opportunities in backward Europe prevented the spread of Muslim influence, and the retreat was inexorable, particularly as Arab political consolidation in the Middle East and Africa broke down, leaving the rulers in Spain isolated. In 1492 CE the last remaining pocket, in Granada, was expelled by the forces of the now-united Spanish monarchy of Ferdinand and Isabella.

At this very time, however, the second Muslim entry into Europe was occurring, in the Balkans. Ottoman Turks systematically conquered this region in the fourteenth and fifteenth centuries, and ruled it for several centuries. Their dominance created a significant Muslim minority, though there were few forced conversions. Muslim immigration

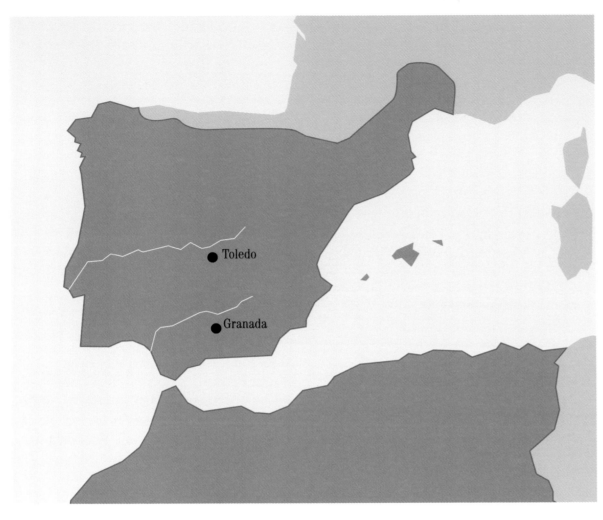

Islam in Spain and France (8th century CE)

from the Middle East plus the activities of Sufi preachers brought many voluntary conversions—as did the higher tax on non-Muslims, particularly in Bosnia. By the mid-sixteenth century, Muslims formed about 20 percent of the population. But trade was limited, and commitments to Christianity remained strong. When the Ottoman Empire began to decline in the seventeenth century, gradually losing territory, the conversion process ceased. A large Muslim minority remained, however, amid frequent hostilities with Christian groups that broke out anew in the late twentieth century. Here, as usual, traditional cultures merged with Islam's influence, creating, for example, the distinctive Bulgarian choral and dance styles applied to Christian and folk themes.

Sub-Saharan Africa

Islam reached Africa south of the Sahara in two ways. Important interactions occurred during the postclassical period, though only a minority of Africans converted (except in North Africa, which religiously merged with the Middle East). But the religious contacts were nonetheless important. They set the basis for much more extensive conversions from the late eighteenth century onward, when missionary efforts and religious wars conducted by fervent Muslims began to spread the religion to ordinary people. By the late twentieth century about 40 percent of all sub-Saharan Africans were Muslim.

Initial contacts in West Africa focused on the Sudanic kingdoms, headed at first by Ghana. These contacts had some distinctive features. Trade with Muslim North Africa developed quickly, across the Sahara Desert by camel and horseback. The trade was vital to Ghana for tax revenues and supply of horses. The king of Ghana also hired Arab Muslims to keep records, because they had writing and bureaucratic experience. But contacts also facilitated raids by Muslims from the north, often encouraged by local Islamic groups.

The kingdom of Mali, which flourished after Ghana collapsed in about 1200, regularized interactions with Muslims. Rulers like Sundiata more systematically utilized Muslim bureaucrats and converted to Islam as a gesture of goodwill toward the North African trading partners. A king of Mali, Mansa Musa, made a famous pilgrimage to Mecca in 1324, dazzling Arabs with his lavish supply of gold. Mansa Musa also organized a center of Muslim scholarship in the city of Timbuktu, and Muslim architecture spread widely. This remained, however, a compromise contact. There was little effort to convert ordinary people, though Sufi missionaries fanned out in the common pattern, with gradual results; their efforts were lim-

ited by the lack of towns south of the Sudanic kingdoms and by disease. In the Sudanic region itself, kings continued to portray themselves as divine, in the West African tradition, despite the contradictions with Islamic faith. And even among the Muslim elite, customs such as giving a relatively prominent place to women persisted, which profoundly shocked Arab visitors, who were otherwise impressed with the culture and political organization they saw around them. Islamic punishments, such as cutting off the hands of thieves, were also rejected as too brutal.

A second strand of Islam stretched down the East African coast, propelled by Arab traders in the Indian ocean. From Egypt, traders and missionaries worked directly southward, in the nation now known as the Sudan (different from the Sudanic kingdoms); beginning with the elite, widespread conversions occurred. Farther south, Swahili merchants—the word in Arabic means "coasters," or people who work along the coasts—established a lively commerce between Indian ocean ports and interior villages. In the process they also brought Arabic language and Muslim religion and political ideas. Many traders intermarried with the African elite, as Islam began to provide cultural unity for upper classes all along the coast. Conversions were voluntary, but Islam represented high social status and the

kind of generalized religion useful to far-flung trade—a religion that local African cultures did not provide. Mosques and other literary and artistic expressions of Islam followed the shift in beliefs, and a mixed Arabic-African language, Swahili, emerged as well, ultimately providing a system of writing as well as facilitating oral communication. The intrusion of Portuguese power in this region in the sixteenth and seventeenth centuries limited further growth, but when Portugal was expelled shortly before 1700 conversions resumed along the trade routes inland.

Central Asia

Central Asia was a vast territory of largely nomadic, herding peoples. It had produced a number of waves of invaders, from the Indo-Europeans to the Huns and Turks, that had affected a variety of regions. Central Asians had also made use of iron and produced key inventions, such as the stirrup, that in turn affected other societies. Buddhism had won some converts, but the area as a whole had remained remote, untouched by many of the currents of the surrounding civilizations.

Islam was the first outside religion to penetrate the region in a systematic fashion, beginning in the eighth century. Most of the region is Muslim today, including the republics that recently broke away from the Soviet Union. The spread of Islam in central Asia involved both of the dominant patterns of Muslim contact: force and persuasion. Arab conquest pressed into Iran and Azerbaijan in the seventh century, and further conquests occurred in Tranoxania, the most settled part of the region, during the eighth century. But there the conquest stopped, and raids between Arabs and Turks ensued. In the ninth century, Muslim traders and then Sufi missionaries began to move out from scattered towns to the nomadic steppes, spreading Islam among the tribal groups. Turkish migrations from central Asia into the Middle East, beginning in the tenth century, further introduced Turks to Islam.

A final stage occurred during the Mongol invasions of central Asia and the Middle East in the thirteenth century. The Mongols were not Muslim, but their conquests brought new contacts between central Asia and the Middle East that in turn completed the conversion of the territory to Islam. In east central Asia, Muslim traders and Sufis made further contacts and conversions, bringing Islam to parts of present-day China such as East Turkmenistan.

As is common with intercultural contact, Islam did not totally alter the established cultures, which continued distinctive forms of art and music, a devotion to imaginative horsemanship, and a relatively high status for women. But conversion did bring change. A key question at the end of the twentieth century involves what kind of Islamic future this region, now free again, will decide to establish.

India

When Islam expanded in the Middle East and central Asia, India was dominated by the older religion of Hinduism. The two faiths differed greatly, as Muslims insisted on subjection to a single god and Hindus believed in a host of specific divinities. Rituals and social beliefs also conflicted. Not surprisingly, initial trading contacts and even successful Arab raids on Indian territory had little cultural impact. A few pockets of Muslims developed, but as small minorities. Hindus largely tolerated these groups. Changes in Hinduism, including more emotional rituals and use of popular languages rather than the scholarly Sanskrit, bolstered this religion's position.

As is common when two major cultures encounter each other, influences moved in both directions. Muslims learned about Indian science and mathematics, including the numbering system that passed to the Middle East (where it was later learned by Euro-

Lands where Islam was spread by Sufi missionaries and traders

→ *Trade routes*

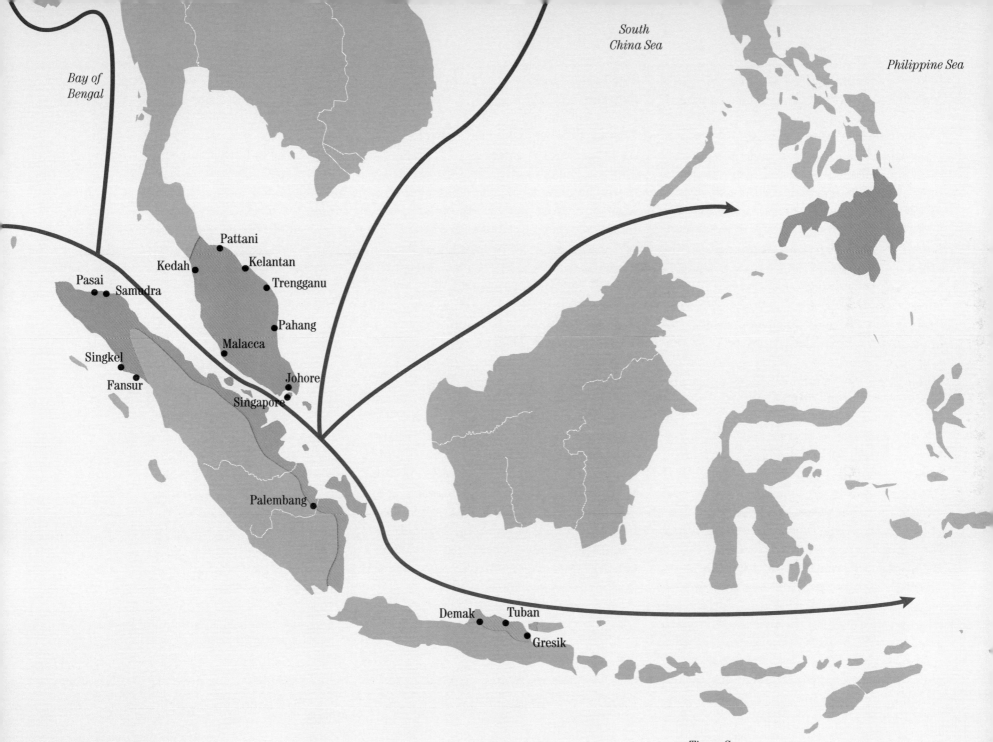

South
China Sea

Philippine Sea

Bay of
Bengal

Pattani

Kelantan

Kedah

Pasai

Samudra

Trengganu

Singkel

Pahang

Malacca

Fansur

Johore

Singapore

Palembang

Demak　Tuban

Gresik

Timor Sea

peans who erroneously called the numerals "Arabic").

The situation changed in the eleventh century, with wider and more durable Muslim conquests in India (spearheaded by Turkish, not Arab, peoples). Turkish conquerors established a large, loosely organized state, the Delhi sultanate, and attacked many Hindu temples and shrines. The stage was set for wider confrontation and contact. Conversions to Islam were encouraged by the presence of a Muslim ruling class, but devout Sufi also poured in, hoping to convert the infidels and winning followers by personal example and merit. Muslim religious leaders also adapted to the cultural setting, using Hindu stories but with Muslim characters and building shrines on the sites of Hindu temples and thus appropriating existing sacred territory. Islam specifically attracted warriors and also people from the lowest castes, drawn by the promise of spiritual equality rather than the Hindu ideas of successive reincarnations. At the same time, a syncretic movement arose within Hinduism, the bhatki cult, that accepted monotheism and spiritual equality—which helped keep some of the lower castes away from Islam proper. Later, in the sixteenth century, when another Muslim empire formed, other Hindu groups developed a new religion from a mixture of Hindu and Muslim principles, notably the Sikhs, who kept many Hindu beliefs but added greater militance.

Overall, however, the main impact of Islam on India was the creation of an important religious minority, in the northwest—closest to the Islamic heartland—but also in the northeast. Most Indians remained satisfied with their own religious culture, and there was no massive immigration of Muslims from other areas. Suspicion of Hindus by Muslim rulers such as those of the Delhi sultanate—who objected to Hindu sensuality and representations of women, which one Muslim writer claimed showed an "essential foulness" in the religion—actually increased loyalty to Hinduism in opposition. Hindu rebellions against Muslim rule, sometimes led by converts to Islam who then changed their minds, also occurred. The difficult relationship between Hinduism and Islam in India—sometimes exhibiting mutual tolerance, sometimes great hostility—continued into modern times, when it was exploited by British colonial rulers, and into the later twentieth century, when it generated tensions between Muslim Pakistan and predominantly Hindu India.

Southeast Asia

This was the last major region affected by Islam, which was introduced during the late fourteenth century. Muslim trading ships from Arabia and particularly from India brought both Muslim merchants and Sufis to the Malay peninsula and the islands that now form Indonesia. Merchants established crucial contacts in the coastal towns, where they influenced the ruling classes. By the fifteenth century, most elites in these cities had been converted. From the coastal towns, Sufis traveled inland, setting up schools and preaching in each village. Islam appealed to inland peoples as a way of integrating with the coastal populations, in a period of expanding trade. By the sixteenth century Islam had become a dominant religion in the Indonesian islands, save for pockets of Hinduism and for isolated, polytheistic peoples in remote parts of the interior. It had won powerful influence on the Malay peninsula and in the southern part of the Philippines. Its spread was stopped only by the arrival of European naval and commercial superiority during the sixteenth century. Even so, it was not pushed back; Indonesia is the largest Muslim nation in the world today.

Islam in southeast Asia inevitably merged with regional cultural influences, including popular costumes, dances, and festivals—including brilliant shadow plays and other pre-Islamic staples based on Hindu epics. The Sufis tolerated large remnants of animist, Hindu, and Buddhist beliefs and rituals—

many of which orthodox scholars would have found contrary to Islamic doctrine. Social relations were governed by pre-Islamic law, and religious law was applied to very specific types of exchanges. Women retained a stronger position than in the Islamic Middle East, often participating actively in market activities. Islam added, in sum, to the mixed, creative culture that predominated in southeast Asia.

Suggested Readings

Ira M. Lapidus, *A History of Islamic Societies* (New York, 1988); Francis Robinson, ed., *The Cambridge Illustrated History of the Islamic World* (New York, 1996). On special areas: Rene Bravmann, *African Islam* (Washington, D.C., 1983); K. N. Chaudhuri, *Asia Before Europe: Economy and Civilization of the Indian Ocean from the Rise of Islam to 1750* (New York, 1990); Avril Powell, *Muslims and Missionaries in Pre-Mutiny India* (Richmond, Surrey, Eng., 1993); Denis Sinor, ed., *The Cambridge History of Early Inner Asia* (New York, 1990).

7. Christianity and the Americas

Europe's regular connection with the Americas, from 1492 CE onward, brought important cultural contacts. Christianity was one of the main European imports to the Americas (which at the time of first contact supported more than a thousand distinct societies), along with new animals, new diseases, and new rulers. Missionary activity was intense. Interest among many previously polytheist native American groups ran high, though Europeans used a mixture of persuasion and force to drive their religion home. Many syncretic combinations developed, even in this unequal interchange. The spread of Christianity also involved Africans brought to the Western Hemisphere as slaves (see Chapter 9).

European religious outreach to the Americas initially involved Catholicism, in part because Catholic Spain and Portugal were the first entrants to American colonization, and in part because Protestant leaders developed an interest in converting local populations more slowly. The missionary surge was part of the same movement that saw new efforts in Asia (see Chapter 5), but the con-

sequences were more sweeping. Later missionary efforts, in the nineteenth century, reached beyond the Americas into Pacific Oceania.

The Catholic church early intervened in Spanish and Portuguese claims in the Americas, sponsoring the 1494 Treaty of Tordesillas that set up respective spheres of influence and arguing that both countries deserved territory in return for bringing the native peoples into the Christian community. Printing presses, imported by the sixteenth century, concentrated heavily on religious materials, while European artistic styles were imported for churches and religious paintings (as well as government buildings). More to the point, religious orders, like the Franciscans and Dominicans as well as the sixteenth-century Jesuit order, provided large numbers of missionaries, establishing churches in the Indian towns and setting up missions in frontier areas. Some early missionaries became ardent defenders of Indian rights. More common were people like Diego de Landa, bishop of Yucatán (Mexico, 1547), who admired Mayans' culture but so

Christianity in the Americas 1500–1700 CE

- ■ Spanish missionary area
- ■ Portuguese missionary area
- ■ French missionary area
- ■ English missionary area
- - - → Missionary routes
- ············ Andes

French

English

Spanish

Portuguese

Mayan culture
(Yucátan Peninsula)

Taki Onqoy
religious movement

Amazon River

detested and feared their religion that he burned all their books and tortured many Indians suspected of backsliding from Christianity. The spread of Christianity in this sense was part of a larger colonial system, a means of institutionalizing conquest and impressing the inferior status of the natives of the Americas.

Missionary outreach was in fact gradual and spotty, even as church structures spread throughout Latin America, the Caribbean, and (by the eighteenth century) up the coast of California. Indian groups in remote areas—for example, parts of the Andes region as well as the Amazon rain forest—long avoided Christianity. Even Indians who entered missions, sometimes eager for protection and interested in European agricultural methods, did not necessarily durably convert.

Still more common were patterns of syncretism, partially concealed in order to avoid government persecution. Attacks on traditional religion and religious leaders, plus the dramatic punishments for nonbelief, left many Indians with few alternatives to conversion, and interest in Christianity was sincere in any event: here was an attractive religion surrounded by the trappings of a powerful society. Yet many Indian and mestizo (Indian-European) groups mixed in old elements as well. During the 1560s, for example, a Taki Onqoy religious movement swept the central Andes of Peru, with native

preachers claiming that the old gods were speaking through them. The preachers argued that spreading disease was a sign of the old gods' displeasure at conversions to Catholicism. Yet many of the priests called themselves Mary or Mary Magdalene, invoking obvious Christian names to add to their appeal. Even after resistance movements of this sort were crushed by colonial authorities, Indians continued to use traditional religious symbols, including family dolls, and combined belief in magic with their Catholicism. Christian prayers and visits to local magicians were used together to deal with disease. In Mexico, Mayan groups combined prayers to the Christian god with agricultural rituals aimed at the traditional gods. Saints in fact represented the older deities, and even the priests found it prudent to overlook this compromise. Christian crosses were commonly covered with the traditional religious cloth, the huipil, which allowed Mayans to worship both sets of divinities together. Easter was less important to the Mayans than was All Souls' Day, because the latter could be merged with traditional ancestor worship, with food offerings placed on the tombs.

The result of Christian outreach in Latin America was a mixed picture. Immigrants of European origin maintained Christian beliefs and also Western artistic and intellectual styles, though they also used some Indian styles and themes (showing colorful

items in church paintings, for example). Mestizos and Indians changed their culture by adopting Christianity and sometimes additional habits, such as a new sense of work discipline and time, and abandoning such older patterns as human sacrifice. But their beliefs were different from pure Europeanism. Added to the mix were African slaves (see Chapter 9), who kept important elements of their culture as well even as they, too, gradually converted to aspects of Christianity. This complex mixture served as the basis for an essentially new Latin American civilization. Its ingredients continued to bubble up even into the twentieth century. By this point, Latin Americans were contributing powerfully to a broader Western culture in literature, art, and music, though with some distinctive emphases. At the same time, new syncretic religions, mixing European, African, and Indian traditions, spread widely, particularly in places like Brazil. In the 1920s, for example, a religion called Umbanda was launched in Brazil, gradually winning millions of believers on the basis of ongoing Indian rituals (including trances) plus Christian and African elements.

North America

Christianity came to North America primarily in the form of European immigration by British Protestants and French and Spanish Catholics. These people brought their religion (and other cultural trappings) with them; in many cases, the desire to practice religion freely was a key motive in coming to the New World, a desire that helped give the European colonies a fervent religious heritage. (To this day, the United States has more widespread religious belief and practice than do most parts of Europe.) Indian populations were far smaller than those in Latin America, and they were soon decimated by disease as well. Pushing the Indians away from the settlements, more than conversion, dominated the thinking of the white settlers. Catholic missionaries were active early on in Canada and other French territories, and in the Spanish missions that spread up the California coast in the eighteenth century; but Protestants showed less interest. Efforts to convert Indians were fitful—Dartmouth College was founded for this purpose in the eighteenth century—and most native American groups retained their own styles and values. White masters also hesitated to Christianize their African slaves, lest education should make them harder to control. Here, however, extensive interaction, including the slaves' learning English, did produce a new cultural mix, and most slave families came to embrace an often fervent Christianity along with elements of their African cultural traditions.

Missionary activity developed in the eighteenth century, but it was often directed at converting existing Christians to a different denomination. Anglicans set up an important effort in 1701, with limited success in Puritan New England. A new group, the Methodists, won many converts, particularly on the colonial frontiers. In the nineteenth century, missionary attempts were extended to Catholic immigrants, again with limited results.

By this point Protestant missionary interest was sufficient to warrant new attention to native Americans. The policy of placing Indians on reservations, which had emerged by the 1830s, had double-edged implications. On the one hand, it got native Americans out of the way of whites, who could then ignore them—or argue, sometimes sincerely, that they were allowing Indians to defend their traditional culture. On the other, reservations were sometimes intended to allow a transition in which missionaries, educators, and other outsiders would "civilize" the natives toward their later integration into the larger American culture. Missionary outreach to the reservations developed steadily, often associated with schools and medical care. Many Indians developed a mixture of Christian and traditional beliefs and rituals. Some, however, simply found their culture eviscerated, with no satisfactory replacement. A fervent revival of traditional religion developed among the Sioux in 1890, with religious visions associated with the "Ghost Dance." Tragically, the movement frightened whites and their attempts to repress it culminated in the Indian massacre at Wounded Knee. The place of native American culture in the United States—indeed, the culture itself—remained a source of contention.

American Christianity was supplemented and altered by steady streams of immigration. New immigration sources in the later nineteenth century brought growing numbers of Catholics and a new Eastern Orthodox minority (along with a smaller Jewish minority and some Muslims). Smaller Asian immigration currents brought some Asian Christians, but also others, who were greeted by missionary efforts that had mixed success. Immigration after World War II augmented Buddhist and particularly Muslim minorities in what was, still, a largely Christian religious culture.

Australia, New Zealand, and Oceania

A final area of Christian conversion emerged in the Pacific in the nineteenth century, with the growing settlement of Australia and New Zealand and increasing contact with the island regions of the Polynesians and other areas. By this point Protestant missionary interest was growing. In Australia and New Zealand, Christianity entered mainly in the ranks of European settlers (though religious sentiment among the new Australians was often muted). Missionaries' attempts among Australian aborigines and the Maoris of New Zealand began fairly early as well. The first mission to the Maoris began in 1814, from Australia. Some Maoris were fully converted, and others mixed Christianity with continued belief in the Maori prophets; the Ratana and Ringati churches maintain this syncretism even today.

Missions in Polynesia followed close on the heels of traders and plantation owners. Close contact with Western advisers convinced Hawaiian kings of the superiority of Christianity, and local polytheist religions were banned in 1819. In 1820 an American Protestant missionary board sent a large contingent to the islands. Conversions followed quickly, along with stringent curtailment of traditional cultural expressions such as the hula. (Catholic missionary efforts, from Europe, also entered in, from 1827 onward, resulting in several years of bitter conflict with Protestant groups backed by the Hawaiian monarchy.) Only in the 1870s was a revival of older styles permitted, along with new imports (from Samoa), such as the grass skirt.

Conclusion

In the Pacific, as in parts of North America, Asia, and Africa, some Christian missionary efforts in the nineteenth century were colored by a pronounced belief in Western superiority, which reduced the flexibility necessary for syncretism. Demands for adherence to Western ways of civilization, including clothing styles, did not prevent substantial conversions, but they also confirmed some groups in their preference for traditional religious and ritual outlets. Thus some American Indians, especially those confined on reservations, largely ignored the missionary appeal. But Christian vigor continued as well. In the later twentieth century, fundamentalist Protestants mounted a huge missionary effort in Eastern Europe, Latin America, and elsewhere, winning important converts. Particularly in places like Guatemala and Brazil, large portions of the population, particularly in the poorer social classes, moved to this new Protestant commitment.

Suggested Readings

Catherine L. Albanese, *America, Religions, and Religion* (Belmont, Calif., 1992); Kenneth S. Latourette, *A History of Christianity* (New York, 1953); Mark A. Noll, *A History of Christianity in the United States and Canada* (Grand Rapids, Mich., 1992); Christopher Vecsey, *On the Padre's Trail* (Notre Dame, Ind., 1996).

8. The Spread of Science

Western Europe's scientific revolution of the seventeenth century had immediate, dramatic implications for Western culture and, in the long run, for cultures around the world. Scientific discoveries about the circulation of the blood or the laws of gravity and planetary motion did more than provide specific new knowledge about the workings of nature. They also generated formal methods by combining generalization, often using advanced mathematics, and empirical inquiry that could advance knowledge still further. And they elevated the position of science and scientific thinking in culture more generally, gradually reducing previous reliance on religious faith.

To be sure, the term Scientific Revolution can be misleading; Steven Shapin argues that there was "no such thing as the Scientific Revolution" in the sense of some fully coherent, standard set of procedures for making scientific knowledge. Scientists did not pursue a single agenda but instead developed an array of cultural practices to understand the natural world. Furthermore, many of the new findings had no immediate practical impact, though some observers, like Francis Bacon in the seventeenth century, confidently predicted that science would lead to technical advances. Discoveries like the circulation of blood had no bearing on medicine until at least the nineteenth century. The accumulation of findings in science did change the intellectual climate in Western Europe, but the phenomenon was complex.

The new European science was not without precedent. China had an old and successful scientific tradition. But in contrast with what came to be called modern science, it relied rather heavily on empirical observations without larger generalizations about nature, and it failed to gain a prestigious place in Chinese culture overall. (Confucianists, particularly, were rarely very interested.) Further, scientific creativity was declining in the seventeenth and eighteenth centuries. The Middle East was center to another active tradition, building on some of the same Greek science that helped spur Western Europe. But Middle Eastern science had receded somewhat in favor of

Early Adopters of Western Science

▦   *Scientifically influential countries visited by high-level Russians, Japanese, and Egyptians*

⟶   *Countries visited by Russians to study Western science*

┈┈┈▸   *Countries visited by Egyptians to study Western science*

⟶   *Countries visited by Japanese to study Western science*

Norwegian Sea

Gulf of
Bothnia

North Sea

Baltic
Sea

RUSSIA
Peter the Great
1697–1698

Sea of Okhotsk

Bay of Biscay

Black Sea

Aral
Sea

Caspian
Sea

1862

Sea of
Japan

to U.S. 1860

Mediterranean Sea

East China
Sea

North Pacific
Ocean

EGYPT
Muhammad Ali
1816

Red
Sea

Arabian Sea

JAPAN
Fukuzawa Yukichi

Gulf of Aden

Bay of Bengal

South China Sea

Philippine Sea

Andaman
Sea

Indian Ocean

Java Sea

Arafura Sea

Timor Sea

Gulf of
Carpentaria

Coral Sea

South
Atlantic
Ocean

Great Australian Bight

Tasman Sea

greater religious fervor from about the twelfth century onward, and hostility to lessons from Christian Europe slowed reactions to advances in the West. For a time, then, the West seemed to stand alone in its new scientific role.

But the power of scientific thinking, and its real or imagined association with other aspects of Western advances, including technology, assured imitation, as other societies became aware of the new developments. Individual intellectuals attracted to innovation, government leaders eager to strengthen their societies through new kinds of training and research—a host of people could be drawn to the new science. Inclusion of novel types of scientific training in school systems, as they developed in the nineteenth and twentieth centuries in the Western world and elsewhere, was a vital step in the reorientation of world cultures.

Ultimately, every society in the world was affected by the power of scientific education and thinking. Science was part of school curricula in every country by the twentieth century, in mass primary education though even more obviously in more advanced training for elites. International student travel to gain science education was another vital facet of cultural contact. Depending on wealth, almost every society produced scientific researchers, whose contacts at inter-national meetings provided one of the key cross-civilization links in the contemporary world. Western influence and the strivings of hosts of new or renewed nations combined to elevate the global impact of science.

But the timing and intensity of interest in Western European science were less uniform than the ultimate results imply. Several societies showed an early awareness. Amateurs in the colonies of North America, for example, began contributing data to European scientists, and by the end of the eighteenth century began some research on their own. In contrast, the Ottoman Empire, in the Middle East, long ignored Western science, admitting some European doctors to the sultan's court in the eighteenth century but otherwise maintaining an isolated stance despite the frequent contacts with Europe.

Three societies suggest some of the patterns of active contact with new European science. Under the leadership of tsar Peter the Great, Russian aristocrats and bureaucrats were urged to gain greater understanding of Western science, technology, and mathematics as part of the "Westernization" program in about 1700. Peter had visited the West several times, including a major trip in 1697–98 to Holland, England, Austria, Italy, and the Vatican. His travels—including an earlier incognito visit when he worked in a Dutch shipyard, convinced him of the need to adopt Western science and technology. Teachers were imported from the West, and aristocrats began to travel in Western Europe and sometimes participate in the scientific discussions that spread widely in elite circles in places like France and England. Academies and societies to support science sprang up in Russia by the 1730s, in imitation of Western models like the British Royal Society. Russia began to be part of a broader scientific community. By the late nineteenth century, Russian scientists, like the physiologist Ivan Pavlov, were contributing major advances to the store of scientific knowledge. Commitment to science continued under communism: by this point Russian scientists ranked among the world's leaders, while science held a vital place in mass education.

Egypt was a second society that sought to import Western science, early in the nineteenth century, in a period when the country effectively split from the Ottoman Empire but before it was taken over by the British Empire. A reformist leader, Muhammad Ali, realized the importance of sending talented students to the West to study, and he also imported teachers. From 1816, students were sent to Italy, France, and England. The result was an important new intellectual current in Egypt and, from Egyptian influence, to other parts of the Middle East, though for some time the impact was less substantial than in Russia.

Japan became aware of Western science in the eighteenth century. While the country was profoundly isolated, contact with Dutch traders in the port of Nagasaki (the only trade connection permitted with the outside world) required a group of translators. This "Dutch school" realized the importance of Western work in science and medicine, and it won some relaxation of prohibitions on the import of foreign books. No major change resulted until Japan was opened to international contacts after 1853, but the presence of the Dutch school, plus Japan's excellent Confucian education system, provided a basis for rapid change thereafter. Hosts of reform-minded officials traveled to the United States and Europe. Leaders like Fukuzawa Yukichi pressed for more scientific training as a key to wider modernization, and they specifically attacked the Confucian tradition. Fukuzawa himself went to the United States as early as 1860, as a personal servant, and then in 1862 served as a translator on a mission to France, England, Holland, Germany, Russia, and Portugal. After 1872, when a national education system was sketched, large numbers of foreigners were imported to teach science. Debates continued about the exact balance between scientific training and more traditional moral education, but sci-ence gained ground steadily. By the twentieth century Japan could boast one of the most scientifically educated populations in the world.

Russia, Egypt, and Japan thus form three case studies of unusually early or unusually intense awareness of Western science—and in two cases particularly, ultimately vital additions to the world's scientific leadership. Their examples must be combined with the broader flows of science that became such a vital part of the twentieth-century world.

The spread of science through deliberate contact with the West did not, of course, produce uniform results or systematic change. As in the West itself, many people combined new scientific beliefs with older practices and rituals. In the field of health, for example, a variety of syncretic mixtures involved consultations with scientifically trained physicians along with traditional medications and religious rituals. The exact place of science in major cultures was not always clear, even at the end of the twentieth century.

Suggested Readings

Evgenii Anisimov, *The Reforms of Peter the Great: Progress Through Coercion in Russia,* John Alexander, trans. (Armonk, N.Y., 1993); Carmen Blacker, *The Japanese Enlightenment: A Study of the Writings of Fukuzawa Yukichi* (Cambridge, Eng., 1964); Alfred Hall, *From Galileo to Newton, 1630 to 1720* (New York, 1982); Stuart Shapin, *The Scientific Revolution* (Chicago, 1996); P. J. Vatikiotis, *The History of Modern Egypt: From Muhammad Ali to Mubarak* (Baltimore, 1991).

9. The African Diaspora

The European discovery of the New World during the fifteenth and sixteenth centuries had profound effects. One of these was the large influx of enslaved African men and women into the European colonies in the Caribbean, South America, and North America. Although the spread of the African populations into the New World is not the only chapter of the African diaspora, it certainly is the most important one. From the time of the ancient Egyptian civilizations, Africans spread into many corners of the world, sometimes as soldiers but mostly as slaves. African culture also spread with the African people, influencing the local culture of the regions where Africans relocated. As a general pattern, however, Africans remained at least partly isolated from the rest of the population and used their cultural values to preserve their identity. This, however, is not to suggest that there was no cultural interchange between the Africans and the non-African population. On the contrary, there is clear evidence that the Africans and the non-Africans culturally influenced one another.

For the purposes of this chapter, only two major segments of the African diaspora will be analyzed: Africans in the world of Islam, and those in the New World (the Caribbean and Latin America [particularly Brazil], and the United States).

The sheer numbers of Africans involved in the slave trades were staggering. Over many centuries, several million people were traded to the Middle East and North Africa—probably about 6 million (estimates range from 4 million to 8 million) between the seventh century and the nineteenth. The Atlantic slave trade was more concentrated, from the sixteenth to the early nineteenth centuries. (A bit earlier, small numbers of slaves had been purchased for plantation labor in Atlantic islands such as the Canaries.) About 12 million Africans were traded to the Americas, though only about 10 million survived to be actually imported there. More than three-quarters of these went to the Caribbean and to South America (particularly Brazil, which took up to 40 percent of the total). Estimates vary,

Trade Routes for African Slaves

→ *Major Islamic trade routes for African slaves (7th–19th centuries CE)*

⇢ *Major European trade routes for African slaves (16th–19th centuries CE)*

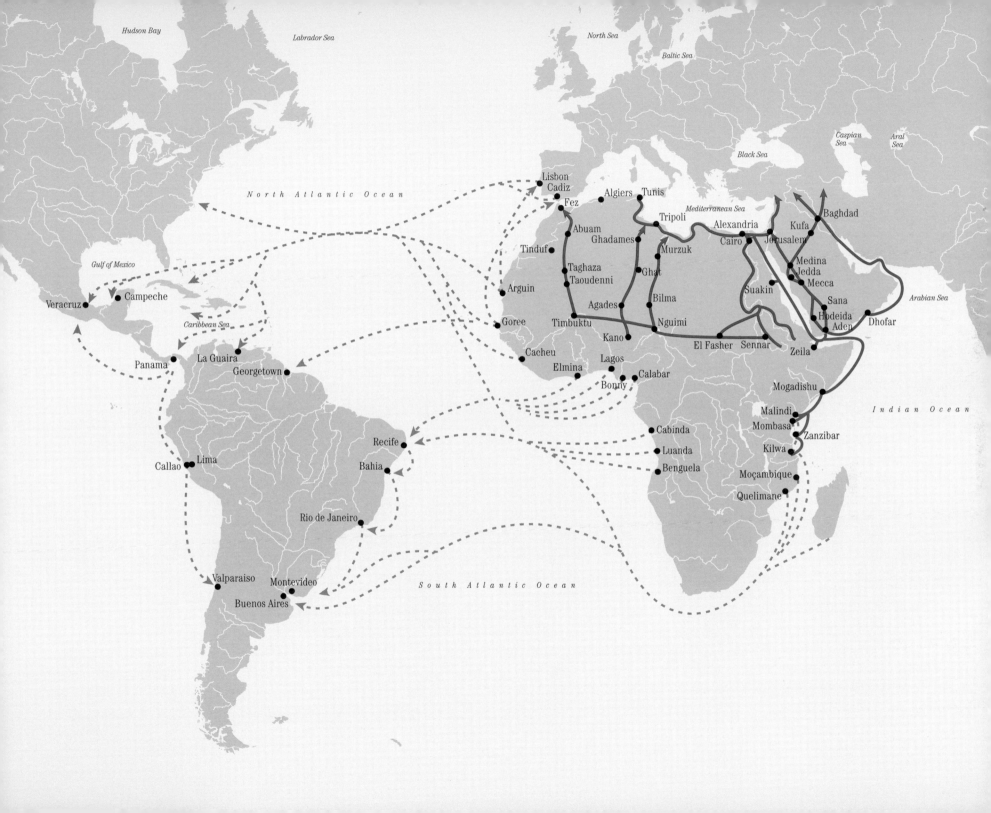

Hudson Bay

Labrador Sea

North Sea

Baltic Sea

Caspian Sea

Aral Sea

Black Sea

North Atlantic Ocean

Lisbon
Cadiz
Fez
Algiers Tunis
Mediterranean Sea
Tripoli
Abuam
Ghadames
Murzuk
Alexandria
Cairo
Jerusalem
Baghdad
Kufa
Medina
Jedda
Mecca

Tinduf

Gulf of Mexico

Veracruz
Campeche

Caribbean Sea

Arguin
Taghaza
Taoudenni
Ghat
Agades
Bilma
Timbuktu
Kano
Nguimi
El Fasher
Sennar
Zeila
Suakin
Sana
Hodeida
Aden
Dhofar

Arabian Sea

Goree

Panama
La Guaira
Georgetown

Cacheu

Lagos
Elmina
Calabar
Bonny

Mogadishu

Malindi
Mombasa
Zanzibar
Kilwa

Indian Ocean

Cabinda
Luanda
Benguela

Moçambique
Quelimane

Callao
Lima

Recife
Bahia

Rio de Janeiro

Valparaiso
Montevideo
Buenos Aires

South Atlantic Ocean

to be sure. British North America received half a million imported Africans; the British Caribbean almost 2.5 million; the French and Dutch Caribbean possessions combined, over 2 million; Spanish Latin America over 1.5 million; Brazil over 4 million. Imports to Latin America were high, both because of extensive need and because of high rates of slave mortality; North American slavery, more severe in some respects, nevertheless encouraged better health conditions and growth through natural population expansion. Thus there were 4 million slaves in the American South by 1860, compared with 6 million elsewhere in the Americas.

Loss of population, but also earnings from the trade, inevitably affected Africa itself. Trade with the Middle East brought funds needed to buy vital goods such as horses. The more concentrated Atlantic trade caused major population loss, particularly because a disproportionate number of slaves were males of child-breeding age (another result was an abundance of women in West Africa). Earnings, however, allowed many African kingdoms to import such new goods as guns but led them to become dependent on profits from foreign exchange. This had political consequences, and it proved disorienting when the trade finally ended as a result of new European policies in the nineteenth century.

But the most important impact of the trade involved the enslaved Africans themselves, and the people with whom they interacted. Not surprisingly, transplanted African people developed a syncretic culture, often a powerful one, in their new homes. Equally important, their culture had measurable impact on the whites who owned them, helping to shape distinctive strains of American culture (both North and South) that continue to define elements of New World identity to this day.

Islamic World

There were African slaves in the Middle East much earlier than the coming of Islam in the seventh century CE. Africans and Europeans had been used as slaves in Roman times. The intensity of the African diaspora into the Middle East, however, increased rapidly during the Islamic era. The Islamic slave trade with sub-Saharan Africa continued for almost fifteen centuries. The cultural influences of this slavery in the Islamic world had some similarities to the patterns later seen in the United States, with a dominant religion tempering imported values. Indeed, lesser racism in the Middle East facilitated cultural assimilation, for Muslims subscribed to the idea of the equality of all believers.

Arab slave traders used the same reasoning as the European slave traders to justify their trade. Africans were regarded as nonbelievers, cannibals and barbarians who deserved to be enslaved. As with Christianity in the United States, the slaves from Africa were quickly converted to Islam. After the conversion, however, the treatment of slaves in the Islamic world was quite humane compared with that in the Americas. The Africans of the Middle East stood a greater chance of being freed, and it was common for an African descendant to climb the social ladder to achieve higher status and some recognition. The only price for these opportunities was complete assimilation into the Islamic religion and culture. The institution of slavery in the Islamic world also contributed to the strong assimilation of the Africans to Islamic culture. Unlike in the New World, the function of slavery in the Middle East was not primarily for production but rather for domestic service. A high proportion of the African slaves were used as servants and office helpers. These slaves were thus highly exposed to the Islamic culture and absorbed all of its components.

Another reason for the intense assimilation of the slaves was the nature of Islam itself. As a religion and culture, Islam was very different from traditional African culture. Islam also was not very tolerant of indigenous cultures and beliefs such as polytheism. Therefore, there was not much chance for African slaves to influence the culture of the Middle East: hence, they were substantially assimilated.

The only exception to this pattern is music, which African slaves carried throughout the diaspora. From the start of the Islamic slave trade to well into the nineteenth century enslaved Africans were used as entertainers and musicians for many social gatherings. Especially during the postclassical period, quite a few African slaves managed to achieve fame and fortune for themselves. After the tenth century, however, this distinctive musical influence of the Africans declined as the music of the slaves became similar to traditional Islamic music.

Overall, the cultural influences of the enslaved Africans on Islamic culture remained small. In this, the situation differed markedly from both of the principal contexts of the Americas, where the greater mass of imported Africans, the attitudes of American whites, and the greater severity of slave labor forged different cultural conditions.

The New World: The Caribbean and Latin America

The main reason for the extension of slavery into the New World was the sugar colonies established by the Europeans. The Europeans had been growing sugarcane with slave labor on the small islands off the coast of Africa since the thirteenth century. After forming colonies in the Caribbean and Latin America, Europeans tried to use the natives of the islands as slave labor on their new sugar plantations. The rate of death among the natives from the diseases introduced by the Europeans (often reaching 80 percent), however, led the Europeans to turn to an old source of slaves, Africa. Slave collection centers were established along the west coast of Africa, although the east coast was also a significant supplier of slaves. In three centuries of slave trade, ships scattered 10 million to 12 million Africans into the New World. The slave ships carried not only men, women, and children but also their gods, beliefs, and traditional cultures. Traces of these African cultural traits still exist in the Caribbean, mostly through syncretism.

The cultural interactions between the African slaves and the European colonials followed similar patterns in Latin America and the Caribbean until the nineteenth and twentieth centuries, as labor needs plus the high death rates of native Americans prompted a desperate quest for imported slaves. Until the nineteenth century, no slave merchant or slave owner would accept the fact that Africans had a culture of their own. Africans were seen as barbaric people who deserved to be slaves. Therefore, what cultural values the slaves had were considered inferior, so the Europeans thought that imposing the culture of the "civilized" world on the slaves was essential. The African slaves in the New World, however, saw integration with European culture as a further subjugation to their masters, and they rejected many attempts to assimilate them to aspects of European culture. Over time, starting in about the eighteenth century, a mentality of preserving mainland African culture became a passive way of resistance for the slaves. The enslaved Africans thought that if they preserved their ancestral culture they would have a bond with mainland Africa. With this, Africans might temporarily escape from rejection and discrimination, hoping to return to Africa one day as free individuals. This idea of cultural isolation prompted the Back to the Roots movement of the nineteenth century, in which a number of recently freed slaves returned to the continent of Africa.

One of the interactions between European and African culture was religious, and many of the slaves in the New World colonies were exposed to Christianization soon after their arrival in the colonies. The belief that the African slaves were inferior, however, eventually prevailed among the clergy in the colonies, and for a century and a half (until the eighteenth century) most of the churches and their services were closed to the slaves: Christianized slaves might become more dangerous, and the idea of holding Christian souls as slaves was uncomfortable. The church services that were open to the Africans did not attract much interest either, as the Africans did not feel comfortable in these lower-class churches. Eventually, some Africans started to see the church as another way of oppression by their masters. Differences between Protestants and Catholics also affected the African experience in the Americas, with Catholics in Latin America initially being more willing to baptize Africans than their Protestant counterparts in what became the United States. This difference both reflected and promoted a lesser degree of outright racism in Latin America, even though material conditions for slaves were often worse than in the North.

Bad conditions, slavery itself, and the hesitations of Christians of European origin did encourage a widespread African desire to use religion as a means of identity and resistance. This was true even after many had converted to Christianity.

Many slaves maintained or reverted to ancestral African religions as a way of preserving their identity and adapting to their social surroundings. In a sense, as the Europeans socially isolated the slaves, the Africans emphasized closer bonding and keeping their identity alive. Therefore, a number of cults and religions started appearing among the slaves in Latin America and the Caribbean; these cults were usually combinations of traditional African religions and Christianity. They were especially dominant in the Catholic colonies, where slaves were economically, socially, and culturally subordinated and alienated. Slaves used these cults to keep their traditional values and to identify themselves with greater forces of the universe rather than with their oppressors. The slaves combined Christian and African values by such practices as worshipping the Christian saints in traditional African ways. Other aspects of European popular religion, such as witchcraft and magic, were combined with traditional African magical beliefs and adapted by the cults of the New World. For example, making a doll or small statue of a person to be cursed (a voodoo doll) had been a common practice in European witchcraft since the Classical Greek times. Examples of these cults are Vodun (or voodoo) in Haiti, Santería in Cuba, Candomble in central Brazil, and Shango in Trinidad and Grenada.

An important influence of the African culture of the New World colonies involved music. Africans' abilities in composition and performance became well known among the European colonials, and African musicians were a common sight during entertainment activities. The music of the Spanish colonies evolved as a unique combination of Spanish and African rhythms. The long domination of Spain by the Muslims left a lasting effect on Spanish music, and these Middle Eastern influences were combined with African music to form the music of the Caribbean. Here was a cultural mix affecting all Americans, regardless of color. Slaves also had profound effects on the language of the New World. The slaves and the masters had to have a common language, so New World languages derived from European languages with heavy African influences. As the islands of the Caribbean became pieces of the larger struggle in Europe, some islands changed hands from one power to another. Therefore the languages of the Caribbean became an interesting mixture of the dominant European language (such as French in Haiti and English in Jamaica) with other European languages (such as Dutch, Portuguese, and Spanish) and African languages. A significant number of African words can be found in every New World nation where people of African descent form either a majority or a significant minority.

Emancipation, spreading in the nineteenth century, did not erase the cultural isolation of the Africans in the Caribbean and in Latin America. In Brazil and other South American countries, Africans remained a minority and stayed culturally isolated in an effort to protect their identity. This racial discrimination solidified the formation of African political and cultural traits, which stressed African culture and struggled to unite the Africans under their common culture and heritage. In Brazil, for example, brotherhoods and other organizations dedicated to the preservation of African culture and identity can be found today. Certain festivals and ceremonies exclusively for people of African descent are still celebrated in some South American countries. These ceremonies and festivals combine European and African patterns—Christian chants are sung to traditional African tunes, for example. Similar trends can be found in Caribbean nations, where Africans struggled to bond together under their common identity in an effort to improve their social conditions. It must be kept in mind that after emancipation people of African descent became the poorest class in these Caribbean nations and colonies. Although emancipation brought social and geographic mobility to some Africans, most were still dependent on whites, who controlled most of the land. As a lower class, Africans still were subjected to rejection and discrimination, and they reverted to cultural isolation to escape these harsh social conditions.

The coming of the twentieth century brought improvements to the descendants of the African slaves in the New World. With industrialization and independence from European powers, an urban middle class was formed among the Africans. These middle classes became influential in the spread of African culture and heritage in the New World. It was during the twentieth century that certain African-influenced New World music was introduced to the world, such as reggae from Jamaica. Overall, however, trends of cultural isolation still exist among the descendants of the African slaves in Latin America. Racial discrimination, economic hardship, and the struggle for equal rights have left Africans still trying to preserve certain cultural traits in an attempt to unify under a common culture.

United States

The case of Africans in the United States stands out as substantially different from that of Africans elsewhere. The slaves in the North American colonies were successfully but incompletely assimilated into European culture over the course of two centuries. It is possible to say that the Anglo-Saxon mentality of North America regarded the African culture in even more derogatory terms than did the Latin mentality of South America and the Caribbean. As a result of this mentality, the traditional cultures and customs of the Africans were suppressed quickly in North America. Regardless of the resistance level of the slaves, many traditional African cultural traits were reduced by the nineteenth century. A good example of the intensity of this cultural assimilation can be seen by comparing the Africans in New Orleans with those in the rest of the United States after the Louisiana Purchase. Africans in Louisiana continued to practice certain traditional religious rituals, such as voodoo and magic, well after 1800, while the pure forms of such traditional cultures had ceased to exist among African Americans elsewhere.

Religion formed the clearest testing ground. White slave owners had hesitated to try to convert Africans, fearing that it might lead to new ideas, as it had in Latin America. But the advantages of having slaves attend white-run churches seemed obvious, so access spread; the main goal (not fully achieved) was to prevent separate black congregations from forming. Africans welcomed Christianity in part because it meshed with traditional ideas about a creator god, but they also inserted their own ingredients: distinctive speech patterns; elements of voodoo; heightened emotionality and chanting, including ecstatic conversion experiences; and references to the burdens of slavery, with emphasis on a dream of freedom. A variety of religious leaders arose spontaneously in slave communities, often hidden from the view of the slave masters. Other white Christian values, such as hostility to premarital pregnancy, were also modified in light of African traditions, which urged family formation and cohesion but on different bases.

As the slaves of North America absorbed Christianity, they saw the church as a temporary escape from rejection and discrimination rather than as a weapon of the oppressors. Instead of forming their culture in isolation, the Africans became an integral part of the urban and rural cultures of the United States, especially in the South. For example, during the period of slavery and even after the Civil War it was common for upper-class southern landowners to have Africans as house servants, positions almost exclusively reserved for older slaves. These servants over time gained the manners and culture of these rich whites. As the slaves (and later free Africans) tended to live together, the cultural traits were passed to other Africans. This example and many others clearly explain the process of cultural assimilation plus preservation of distinctive styles and values among the Africans in the United States, despite the burdens of slavery and white racism.

After the Civil War and the emancipation of the slaves, the cultural status of African Americans started to improve. With emancipation came geographical mobility, which resulted in many waves of black migrations to the North, Midwest, and West. Gradually, the culture of African Americans started to influence the popular culture of the United States, even beyond the South. During the period of slavery, the folk culture of the African slaves had become the general folk culture of the entire South. Despite its racial biases, the upper class of the South accepted many elements of the rich, humorous folk culture of the Africans. Slave songs from the period, along with folk tales and such, were popular in the South, even among the whites. After emancipation and the spread of Africans to the whole of the United States, this black folk culture became an integral part of the American culture. Although segregation and discrimination still prevented most Africans from being heavily involved in the elite arts—like play writing, sculpture, and painting—popular arts like music and dance were heavily influenced by the culture of the Africans. The deep impact of jazz and ragtime on American culture demonstrates the far-reaching involvement of people of African descent in the development of the United States. Soon, popular arts and sports also became ways for many African Americans to compete with whites, and African Americans became heavily involved in these areas. From the late nineteenth century onward, African American writers, artists, and composers have sought to convey black values and ways of life to a wide audience, while religious and, later, political and business activities expanded.

Substantial cultural mixing did not bring full integration, just as it did not bring social or economic equality. Even aside from special pockets of African cultures, on some of the islands off South Carolina and in Louisiana, where African dialects might persist, African Christianity often had an emotional enthusiasm and a distinctive gospel music that mixed the new religion, African identity, and the slave experience. Food selections were similarly syncretive, preserving a special African American cuisine.

Although interest in an African identity and in the advancement of the black people carried on in the African American culture, these cultural aspects are closer to the general American culture than to the traditional African culture of the slaves. The cultural relationships between Africans and non-Africans of the United States were by no means one-sided. Africans did assimilate many cultural values of whites—including vivid hopes for individual mobility and success, though these hopes were often dashed. But the influence worked both ways. Although not recognized at the time, the culture of the slaves and their descendants contributed greatly to the white culture, forming many American styles we see today.

Conclusion

African culture had powerful persistence. Deeply rooted religious beliefs, connecting Africans with their environment through worship of ancestors and gods of nature, including a creator god, combined with strong community and family ties. Transmission by story and memory, in a largely oral tradition, added to the mix. But the African diaspora operated under unusual force and hardships. People were torn from familiar associations, mixed with Africans from other regions, compelled to endure a hideous, disease-filled journey, and then to work as slaves for scornful masters. Small wonder that many cultural elements disappeared, though scholars have uncovered far more powerful survivals and confirmations than was once realized. A variety of combinations were possible, depending on the pressures and opportunities provided by the slave owners. Assimilation prevailed in the Middle East, creative persistence and syncretism in the Caribbean and Latin America, with the United States providing a complex case in between.

Suggested Readings

Martin Kilson et al., eds., *The African Diaspora: Interpretive Essays* (Cambridge, Mass., 1976); Lawrence Levine, *Black Culture and Black Consciousness* (Oxford, 1977); Ronald Segal, *The Black Diaspora* (New York, 1995); Mechal Sobel, *The World They Made Together: Black and White Values in Eighteenth-Century Virginia* (Princeton, N.J., 1987); Vincent Thompson, *The Making of the African Diaspora in the Americas* (Harlow, Essex, Eng., 1987).

Part III
The Modern Centuries

The past two and a half centuries of world history have been marked by two major changes in the nature of cultural contacts, though important similarities to past episodes remain important as well. First, progressive acceleration in international commerce and in transportation and communications technology brought societies into closer contact than ever before; this acceleration also opened relationships among parts of the world unaccustomed to such diverse sources of cultural influence. Particularly during the nineteenth century, these developments were supplemented by the wave of European and U.S. imperialism, which force-fed certain cultural features to a host of societies in Asia and Africa. The second major development involved the emergence of belief patterns that differed from previous religious and artistic currents. Some of these patterns, like Marxism, were supported by eager advocates who essentially took on a missionary role. Most emphasized a this-worldly, secular focus, whether on social revolution (like the Marxists) or on an attachment to a nationalist state.

There were two further results of these changes. First, some kinds of cultural contacts began to reach significantly into popular behavior, reflecting values and styles that often seemed to diverge strikingly from traditional patterns. Thus the spread of international sports interests and consumer culture, particularly from the late nineteenth century onward, involved adjustments of personal tastes and habits to global influences. Second, many areas sought to use values learned from Western models to help defend regional identities. Nationalism spread much like other secular belief systems, but it ironically helped people resist other international influences in the name of regional pride and superior values. The nationalist result of cultural contact, in fact, deserves careful attention. The idea resulted from interactions with Western Europe and the United States (though nationalism also spread from successful movements in other parts of the world; thus the success of places like India helped inspire nationalism in Africa). Cultural contact did prompt nationalists to urge reforms in their own countries, to bring them closer to Western levels of power, if nothing

else. But nationalism also encouraged resistance to cultural contact, sometimes inducing growing intolerance as well as pride in real or imagined regional beliefs and styles. The most recent chapters of cultural contacts in world history hardly suggest a uniform process of homogenization but rather a mixture of embrace and recoil.

In this section I deal with several kinds of cultural contact, mostly emanating from Western Europe and the United States to other parts of the world, where, however, the influences would be diversely accepted and interpreted—as has always been the case in world history. Contacts not only involved formal beliefs, like Marxism, but also more subtle cultural systems, like gender distinction. It is also important to note reverse flows: the pattern of artistic influences in the later nineteenth century shows how the West could still be affected by compelling cultural currents from other societies, as contacts opened up new vistas for Westerners as well.

The power position of the West in many modern cultural contacts invites careful scrutiny. Many European and American leaders, confident of their own values, looked down on other cultures and assumed that their own beliefs should increasingly be embraced. But Western models spread unevenly, despite increasing interaction in trade and the power of new technologies, such as films, television, and computer links, to accelerate exchange. The recourse of syncretism remained important; few cultures, if any, simply tried to become Western without qualification. Resistance and complex combination, in fact, remind us that modern cultural contact retains important similarities with earlier exchanges in world history.

10. The Spread of Nationalism

The worldwide spread of nationalism from the late eighteenth century to the early twentieth century resulted from two kinds of cultural contact. One was hostile: as Western influence and imperialism spread, many peoples sought movements that would maintain or reassert their independence and cultural integrity. Nationalism, couched in terms of liberation from the West, proved ideal here. But nationalism also spread from the West, where it had begun. Many areas adopted nationalism because of its success in organizing European states and because it spoke a language that Europeans might respect and understand. Nationalism, in other words, resulted from new cultural connections even as it commonly asserted resentment against too much internationalism and outside influence.

The dependence of nationalism on new contacts created a clear chronology. Areas in active touch with Western Europe embraced nationalism first, in an initial wave between 1800 and 1848. This early nationalism was usually pro-Western and sought to imitate Western trends and to cultivate Western support. Later, between the 1870s and the 1930s, nationalism spread to Asia and Africa, usually in a more complex mixture of anti-Western but imitative elements.

Nationalism appealed to old passions, but it was a modern political culture, newly appearing in the last half of the eighteenth century. Traditional loyalties had usually focused on family and kin groups; regions or regional states; and/or religions. They might be fierce, distinguishing between one's own group identity and that of outsiders, but they were not normally national. Nationalism involved beliefs in a common culture (sometimes associated with a dominant ethnic group) and, usually, in a state that should embody and celebrate that culture. National units were larger than most regions; they subsumed kinship or tribal loyalties. At the same time, national passions were more secular than were most religions. Nationalisms were, in sum, rather new inventions of modern world history, replacing or at least modifying older loyalties. And the emotions that nationalism might inspire could be intense.

Spread of Nationalism in Europe, Africa, and Asia

■ *Nationalism first appeared 1789–1847*

■ *Nationalism first appeared 1848–1914*

□ *Nationalism first appeared 1914–present*

Two key features of nationalism complicate basic definitions. First, while nationalism did spread from its initial center in Western Europe, it was obviously not just a result of cultural contact. Each nationalism proclaimed distinctive features of its home unit. More than with most results of contact, as a result, nationalisms varied greatly from one site to the next, depending among other things on inspirational individual leaders. Second, nationalisms always incorporated a subtle mixture of tradition (including invented traditions) and impulses for change. Nationalists had to find some cultural traditions to praise, as an indication that their nation was indeed distinctive, worth identifying and liberating. At the same time, nationalists also had to modify purely traditional loyalties and other barriers to national strength and unity. Nationalists might thus proclaim the beauties of a customary majority religion while seeking to import more effective medical or industrial practices that pointed in new cultural directions. The combination of identity and reform helps account for nationalism's frequent strength and impact.

Early Stages: Nationalism's Emergence and Initial Spread

National monarchies had existed for some time in Europe, in France, England, and Spain, for example, but they did not initially focus clear-cut national beliefs. Nationalism began to emerge in the eighteenth century. Certain intellectuals, like Johann Gottfried von Herder in Germany, reacted against the cosmopolitanism of the Enlightenment, arguing that different nations had distinct characters as a result of organic history. Merchants, seeking to profit from widening markets, were attracted to the idea of the nation as a commercial unit, within which free trade might occur but which might also protect against foreign competition; nationalism was early associated with a rising middle class, as against older aristocratic identities. The French Revolutionaries, who argued that the state had direct contact with its citizens, encouraged nationalist passions, including the first national anthem and one of the first national (as opposed to royal or regional) flags. French armies inspired nationalist commitments in opposition to their invasions, particularly in Spain, Italy, and Germany; and English nationalism was also furthered in the battles against the hated French. Though conservatives continued to attack nationalism in the name of older dynastic states and religion, nationalism gained ground steadily in Western and Central Europe during the early decades of the nineteenth century. It ultimately helped inspire the unification of Italy and Germany and the creation of the Belgian national state.

Beaufort Sea

Baffin Bay

Bering Sea

Gulf of Alaska

Hudson Bay

Labrador Sea

North Pacific Ocean

North Atlantic Ocean

Gulf of Mexico

Caribbean Sea

South Pacific Ocean

South
Atlantic Ocean

From its initial center, nationalism spread to other areas with trade and cultural contacts with Western Europe. Full-blown nationalism did not figure directly in the American Revolution, as distinct from a desire for self-government and independence from England. But efforts to create and justify an effective new state began to produce, by the early nineteenth century, clear statements of American nationalism, along with rituals, such as the celebration of July 4, and symbols, such as Uncle Sam. The example of both U.S. and French revolutionary nationalism spread to aspiring political leaders like Simón Bolívar in Latin America, who argued against Spanish rule on the basis of rights of national self-determination. The identities of Latin American nations were not entirely clear, and several early units collapsed in internal strife, but the nationalist concept was firmly planted in the wars of independence between 1810 and 1820.

Nationalism spread even more clearly to eastern and southeastern Europe, other areas with active trading ties to Western Europe. Merchants led claims to national freedom against Ottoman rule in Serbia before 1810. Greek nationalism spread, again against Ottoman control, leading to a major independence war at the end of the 1820s that won great sympathy in Western Europe and in Russia. Slavic nationalists began to create collections of national stories and language dictionaries, leading by the 1830s and 1840s to demands for political independence for such areas as Czechoslovakia and Poland (where a number of rebellions were put down).

The first spread of nationalism produced a mixture of integrating and disintegrating efforts. Nationalists in the new United States, or in Germany, proclaimed the political integrity of large units, as against smaller states, such as Bavaria, or distinctive regions, like the American South. Nationalists in much of Eastern Europe, however, attacked large units because they were multinational. Nationalism in the Balkans, particularly, identified a host of small ethnic cultures that are fiercely proclaimed and defended to this day. Latin American nationalism took a somewhat middle ground, attached as it was to such fairly large states as Argentina, but it was unable to defend more ambitious federations in Central America or in the northwestern part of South America.

The first round of nationalism did, however, share a key characteristic: it was normally attached to broadly liberal political values. Nationalists fought for parliaments and constitutions as well as for national independence. Only gradually did it become apparent that conservatives might embrace nationalism as well, as a vigorous loyalty that could be invoked to defend existing states. The Argentine strongman leader Manuel de Rosas used nationalism to defend his authoritarian rule in the 1830s. Germany's Otto von Bismarck linked nationalism to a strong, conservative state by the 1860s. Nationalism also spread to Russian conservatives, who were eager to appeal to Russian identity in order to protect the beleaguered tsar. Conservative nationalists in Russia were also among the first to define an anti-Western nationalism, arguing that Russia should stop imitating Western values, which were chaotic, secular, and materialist, and instead defend the communal and religious traditions that made Russia a superior state.

The Spread of Nationalism to Asia and Africa

The second phase of nationalism's spread depended directly on increasing European penetration of Africa and Asia. European imperialists and merchants gained ground in the two largest continents as aggressive representatives of nations, not of Western society as a whole. From colonial governors and traders, and later educators, Asian and African leaders learned the importance of being British or French or German, and could easily begin to think in similar terms for their own societies. Nationhood meant strength. At the same time, purely traditionalist resistance to European penetration seemed inadequate, poorly armed and, often, disunited. To be sure, important restatements of Hinduism and Islam occurred by the 1850s, as one reaction to European influence and arrogance, but these did not seem to address sufficiently the growing power imbalance. Nationalism could be more explicitly tied to issues of military improvement and state efficiency.

Nationalism began to emerge in parts of the Arab world by the 1870s. As early as the 1860s Christian merchants in Lebanon, with unusually active trade and cultural ties with Europe, launched Arab nationalism—on a basis similar to nationalism's spread to the Balkans earlier on, including new inquiries into past national culture. Elsewhere, as in Egypt, nationalism was more commonly headed by journalists and lawyers who, as a result of earlier, more limited reform movements, had been partially educated in the West. Egyptian nationalist Mustafa Kamil, for example, held a French law degree. Some Jews and Christians also participated, eager for a movement that would be inclusive. Nationalists initially focused on speeches and newspaper articles, but by the 1890s they were forming political parties in places like Egypt. Arab nationalists began to sponsor comprehensive meetings during the early years of the twentieth century, in protest against Ottoman control and in the interest of forming new, independent nations like Iraq.

Turkish nationalism also developed in the region. The Ottoman Empire sponsored elaborate military training and advice from Germany. A number of army officers were sent to Europe for schooling. From this mix came specific movements to go beyond mere reforms of the Ottoman system, to a nationalist-based Turkish state. The nationalist Young Turks, as they were called, agitated strongly before World War I and then, in the chaos after the war, seized the initiative to create a separate Turkey, dedicated to national independence but also to a host of Western-style reforms.

Educated Indians, mostly from the top castes and often employed in the lower or middle ranks of the British colonial government, spearheaded Indian nationalism. An initial Indian National Congress met in 1885, with modest demands for more Indian representation in the bureaucracy. From this base nationalism spread rapidly among the elites, particularly Hindus. Many leaders were directly educated in the West under colonial policies that depended on trained local personnel to help administer far-flung domains that British imperialists might direct but could not largely staff. Mohandas Gandhi, for example, who became the key nationalist leader from the 1920s until independence in 1947, was educated as a lawyer in London and also gained experience in South Africa. From his experience he acquired a fierce devotion to Indian independence and the superiority of key Indian values, but also an insistence that, in the name of nationalism, certain Western ideas had to be applied as well: such as the abolition of the caste system in favor of equality under the law for all citizens.

Nationalism also emerged in Japan in the 1880s, but there under government sponsorship after a period of vigorous Westernization. During the 1870s large numbers of Western advisers had poured into Japan, staffing and administering much of the growing school system, among other duties. Conservative officials, including the emperor, worried that Western individualism and other corrosive values might damage Japanese culture, and they called on nationalism, supplemented by a revived Shinto religion and other, partially invented traditions, to support more assured loyalty to state and hierarchy. Nationalism began to be used to motivate higher production, economic sacrifices, and other qualities that helped propel rapid development; it soon sparked a new imperialism as well.

Nationalism spread more slowly to places like Indonesia, but by 1900 cultural groups were forming to protect or revive older traditions. Indonesians educated in Dutch schools played a leadership role here. The groups gradually developed more political goals, and after World War I they formed an outright independence movement.

Nationalism was also late in Africa, in part because European conquest came late, and in part because most of the colonial units were arbitrary, with no relationship to political tradition. North Africa, taken over by French and Italian forces, produced branches of Arab nationalism by 1900. Below the Sahara, individual Africans began to formulate new bases for demands for rights—after purely traditional resistance had failed—at about the same time. John Sarbah (1865–1910) from the British Gold Coast colony (now Ghana) was the first West African admitted to the English bar, after legal education in England. He argued for customary laws and communal virtues, though he did not develop a full nationalist statement. Only in the 1920s and 1930s did a larger number of Africans, trained in Western schools, often with a stint in London or Paris (or at a U.S. university), produce more sweeping nationalist agitation. The first meeting of the Pan-African National Congress occurred in 1919.

For many Asians and Africans, World War I was a crucial lesson in nationalism. European nations fought the war for nationalist goals, and observer-participants like the Japanese saw no reason that their nationalist ambitions should not advance as well. French and British governments used large numbers of African and Indian troops as part of their war effort; the experience of fighting in Europe helped drive home the meaning of nationalism. The British encouraged Arab (and Jewish) nationalism in the Middle East, hoping to undermine the Ottoman Empire, which had sided with Germany. Contact in war, after contact in empire, schools, and trade, set the seal on a steady increase of nationalist agitation and identification through much of the twentieth century.

Conclusion

Nationalist passions persist at the end of the twentieth century. Ironically, most nations as units have been displaced economically by the surge of larger international trading forces, ranging from powerful multinational companies to new trade blocs such as the European Union or treaties like the North American Free Trade Agreement (NAFTA). At the same time, some leaders have decided that nationalism fails to provide enough protection for key values. Thus a revived

Muslim movement, in places like Iran, looks more to religious fervor than to classic nationalism to keep undesirable foreign cultural influences at bay, while a growing Hindu National party blends nationalism with religion in ways that earlier nationalist leaders might have deplored. Yet nationalism still burns bright, and there are some powerful recent statements. Several regional nationalisms—in places like Quebec, Scotland, and Catalonia—have gained new life under the umbrella of supranational trading blocs, playing off new multinational agencies against their own national capitals. The collapse of the Soviet Union and Yugoslavia, by 1991, also unleashed new nationalist passions in Eastern Europe and central Asia. Nationalism has been one of the key cultural-political responses to unprecedented contacts in modern world history, but the forces it has represented have always been complex, and its future is unclear.

Suggested Readings

Benedict Anderson, *Imagined Communities: Reflections on the Origin and Spread of Nationalism* (London, 1983); Ernest Gellner, *Nations and Nationalism* (Ithaca, N.Y., 1983); Florencia Mallon, *Peasant and Nations: The Making of Post Colonial Mexico and Peru* (Berkeley, 1994); Hugh Seton-Watson, *Nations and States: An Enquiry into the Origins of Nations and the Politics of Nationalism* (London, 1977); Anthony Smith, *The Ethnic Origins of Nations* (Oxford, 1986).

11. Imperialist Ideas About Women

Gender relations often reveal some of the most intense beliefs of a society because they reach so deeply into private lives, personal identities, and power arrangements. At the same time, substantial contacts between societies often bring some awareness of different gender standards. The result may lead a society—at least a society open to influence—to modify prior traditions, or it may call forth resistance to possible change as gender becomes one of the areas defended as integral to the preservation of cultural integrity.

Prior episodes of cultural contact often had implications for gender issues. Japanese imitation of China, in the postclassical period, brought in stricter ideas about women's inferiority, which affected patterns in Japan, though not to the same level of inequality that prevailed in China. Muslim travelers in Africa were concerned about African traditions of considerable freedom for women—because Africans, even in sincerely converting to Islam, did not hew to the gender standards more common in the Middle East.

The spread of Western colonies in the nineteenth century brought clear challenges to local gender traditions, particularly where the treatment of women was concerned, from Africa to Polynesia. Europeans, convinced of their superiority in any event, had very strong beliefs about the appropriate place and treatment of women. They often judged African or Asian customs harshly. Their views, sometimes backed up in colonial laws and often illustrated by the presence of a minority of European women in the colonies, as wives of officials and planters but also as missionaries, inevitably influenced the people with whom they came into contact.

As European powers raced each other to colonialize, governments, missionaries, and volunteer services struggled to spread selected European values to the indigenous peoples of these lands. Over time, the status of women in the colonies came to represent the success of the Europeans' quest to "civilize" their colonies. Therefore, a significant amount of attention was paid to the status and role of women in the colonies. European colonial governments and missionaries tried

European Influence on Gender in Africa and India, 19th and 20th Centuries

– – – ➔   *Trade routes between Asia, Africa, Europe, and U.S.*

▨   *Areas colonized by European powers*

▬ ▬ ▬ ➔   *Approximate area affected by Indian Mutiny, 1857*

•   *Main centers of Indian Mutiny*

FRANCE

PORTUGAL   SPAIN

Black Sea

GREECE

*Caspian
Sea*

TUNISIA
(French)

Mediterranean Sea

NW PROVINCES

MOROCCO
(French)

Meerut
Bulandshan
Dehli
Bareilly
Aligarh
Fategarh
Agra
Lucknow
Mainpuri
Kalpi
Gwalior
Allahabad
Jhansi

ALGERIA
(French)

LIBYA
(Italian)

EGYPT
(Ottoman
dominion under
British control)

*Persian
Gulf*

RIO DE ORO
(Spanish)

*Red
Sea*

*Gulf of
Oman*

INDIA

*Arabian
Sea*

GAMBIA
(British)

FRENCH WEST AFRICA

ANGLO-EGYPTIAN
SUDAN

ERITREA
(Italian)

FRENCH
SOMALILAND

*Bay
of Bengal*

RTUGUESE
NEA

BRITISH
SOMALILAND

*Andaman
Sea*

LIBERIA

GOLD
COAST
(British)

NIGERIA
(British)

SIERRA LEONE
(British)

TOGO
(German)

CAMEROONS
(German)

ETHIOPIA

ITALIAN
SOMALILAND

Indian   Ocean

*Women's War (1929)
Protesting taxation
by the British
colonial
administration*

RIO MUNI
(Spain)

FRENCH
EQUATORIAL
AFRICA

UGANDA
(British)

BRITISH
EAST AFRICA

BELGIAN
CONGO

GERMAN
EAST
AFRICA

NYASALAND
(British)

ANGOLA
(Portuguese)

NORTHERN
RODESIA
(British)

MOZAMBIQUE
(British)

MADAGASCAR
(French)

GERMAN
SOUTH
WEST
AFRICA

SOUTHERN
RHODESIA
(British)

BECHUANALAND
(British)

*South
Atlantic   Ocean*

UNION OF
SOUTH AFRICA
(British)

*Zimbabwe (1999)
Women's rights to
property must be
inferior to those of men*

*South Africa (1956)
20,000 women march
protesting the extension of
the apartheid pass laws
to African women*

to impose imperial ideas of gender in these indigenous societies, which produced mixed results. In some places, European ideas about women were readily accepted by the locals, and in other places there was considerable resistance to these European values. Furthermore, in some areas European ideas about women were combined with local ideas, which formed a distinctive set of tensions for women in these societies.

One reason for these mixed results was the complexity within the European societies concerning gender. European (especially Victorian) values for women emphasized domesticity and a more important public role for men. At first, colonies were declared to be "no place for a white woman," and European women were not permitted to travel to them. Later, when travel was permitted, white women were encouraged to do missionary work to spread Victorian European values among the inhabitants of the colonies. The result was anomalous: powerful women, often critical of "native" gender practices, preached ideas about women's domesticity. Small wonder that the outcome was a set of mixed gender values in the colonies. Europeans might undermine local customs that protected women within a larger family community because of their belief that women should be identified as part of a husband-headed household, even when they also attacked husbands' abuse of their power. Concern about the presumed sexuality of many "native" peoples also led to efforts to restrict women's rights in public, in colonial settings. The available European example was complex.

Furthermore, Europeans did not necessarily push for massive change in the local relationships between men and women. They were concerned with power and profit far more than with reform, and often their interests dictated collaboration with male dominance (which they agreed with in any event, in some respects). Even when they did push for change, the motive might be to undermine local male authorities, as part of the whole imperialist enterprise, rather than to benefit women explicitly. Cultural contact could allow local women to gain some perspective on traditional beliefs and practices concerning their sex, but they would often have to oppose colonial restrictions to gain greater leeway. Ultimately, it was what local men and women took from their interactions with European models that counted, just as in cultural contacts in other respects. Historians are vigorously debating how this all worked out, including what Europeans themselves intended, where gender issues were concerned.

Two key places in which European influences strongly affected the history of gender issues are India and Africa, which can serve as case studies for the wider phenomenon. The two cases also encourage comparison: European values could have different impacts on colonial societies, depending on specific European attitudes, prior regional traditions, and ongoing economic change.

India

British colonial rule in India gave a significant amount of attention to the role of women in Indian society. During the 1860s the British colonial administrators of India declared the status of indigenous women to be a measure of "civilization," and many European and American missions started efforts to impose a "civilized" role for women in Indian society. These missions usually began in the coastal regions and gradually spread inland and northward during the late nineteenth and early twentieth centuries. The foremost priority of these missions was to convert indigenous women to Christianity. Missionary women preached and sang religious songs, both in public and in the private residences they were invited to. Apart from religious duties, the European missionary women emphasized domestic obligations. They did simple nursing and taught domestic skills to Indian women. They stressed the importance of couples doing social activities together, rather than participating in segregated activities within

lems within African communities, and ev
tually a resistance to Victorian gender ide
arose among Africans.

It must be noted that some of the mot
tions of Europeans to "domesticate" Afr
women were much different from thos
the case of India. In Africa, the statu
women was not taken as a measure of
lization in the colonies. New regulat
were introduced to protect the Europ
population in sub-Saharan Africa. Afr
women were seen as being sexually se
tive, as their dresses revealed much of t
bodies. Over time, a prejudice was for
that the high regard for sexuality in Afr
society also corrupted the European po
tion, which became more sexually a
than the Europeans back home. For e
ple, the British abandoned their pra
of sending single, female nurses to
Africa, because of presumed sexual ten
tions. In another development, amid fea
African sexuality—part of the Euro
racial stereotype—European dress wa
posed on African women in an effort to
sexual provocation. Except for the u
elite, African women mostly rejected
European styles, as they were impracti
daily African life.

The European impact on Africa proved
ly disruptive to gender relationships.
nomic developments, pulling or forcing

their houses. The missionaries' main goal
was to impose Victorian ideas of women on
Hindu society, thereby teaching the merits
of European civilization.

An important issue, both for missionaries
and British colonial administrators, involved
divorce and widowhood among Hindu and
Muslim families. In both types of families
women were not allowed to divorce and widows were not allowed to remarry. And because women were not allowed to own
property, except in marriage, the widows
lived in poverty for the rest of their lives.
The Europeans' approach to this problem
shows the effects of Victorian domestic values in the colonies. Instead of struggling to
give women property rights, the Europeans
tried to overcome the problem by supporting
remarriage for women. This was a safe way
to get property and was in accordance with
Victorian domestic values, which stated that
the place of a woman was by her husband's
side, doing domestic work. The remarriage
law of 1853 was designed to solve this problem. It attracted so much resistance from
the Indian population that it figured among
the reasons for the mutiny of 1857.

British colonial administration also adopted
other laws and regulations that enforced the
idea of domesticity on indigenous women.
During the late nineteenth century, a law
was passed that gave the husband the right

to force his wife to remain in the couple's
home. Prior to this law, Hindu tradition stated that a married woman could live with her
parents if there were problems with the
marriage and the wife was forced to leave.
The British strongly believed that an Indian
woman's place was with her husband at
home and that the domesticity of women
should be achieved at any cost. As seen from
these examples, the British colonial government and European missionaries, although
trying to improve the status of Indian
women in some respects, also imposed new
restrictions on them.

Indian feminists of the late nineteenth century also strongly opposed arranged mar-
riages of young girls to older men. Overall,
Indian women criticized the sexist ideas of
both Indian and European societies, along
with those of the three competing religions: Hinduism, Islam, and Christianity. A
small but vigorous group of Indian missionaries gave Indian women a sense of femi-
nism that was based on Indian values rather
than on pledging allegiance to European culture, which seemed "civilized" on the surface
but proved equally discriminating against
women.

Two kinds of tensions formed amid British
influence on India: the first involved Indian
women educated in Christian schools, some
of them converts to Christianity, who found

British models inadequate; the second, pushing in a different direction, involved Indian
nationalists, led by men, who viewed for-
eign-influenced change in gender roles with
some suspicion.

Some educated Indian women began to visit
Britain and were upset by the gender segregation of British society. Returning
home, they at once fought Indian gender
traditions and important aspects of the
British example. To the chagrin of missionary leaders, they taught "masculine skills,"
such as carpentry and masonry, to fellow
Indian women. They also stressed "Indian-
ness" in dress and behavior, rejecting the
European customs that the missionaries
were trying to impose. At the same time
they tried to insist on breaking down caste
barriers for Hindu women, arguing that
lower-caste women should have the same
privileges in marriage as the upper castes.
They sought greater power for women in
such areas as divorce and property owner-
ship while promoting self-sufficiency for di-
vorced women and widows. Here were important spurs to change that have continued
to influence Indian society, particularly
among the better-educated groups. A sense
of women's rights different both from tradition and from European models informs
gender developments in India to this day.

12. The Development of International Art

Many nationalist movements praised a
pects of gender traditions in India. Th
made halting gestures toward more forr
education for women, even in the upr
castes, while stressing domestic subje
and roles. Ideas about women's inferior
persisted, while Victorian notions of spe
female virtue did not penetrate. Practi
such as arranged marriage were vigorou
defended as part of the national and r
gious heritage. In addition, of course, m
women, particularly in the countryside, w
not touched by Western influence one v
or another.

On balance, Western-sponsored laws a
ideas had complex impacts on India, cr
ing new divisions and tensions while ur
niably spurring significant changes am
some groups and individuals.

Sub-Saharan Africa

After the "scramble" for Africa was ove
the end of the nineteenth century, Europ
powers had partitioned most of sub-Sa
ran Africa. The indigenous women of s
Saharan Africa won much attention, t
from the Europeans and the colonial g
ernments, but the reason for this atten
was much different from the case of Ir
The European view of African women
in accordance with the deep prejudice

Cultural contacts in the modern period
often featured Western influences on other
societies, but international exchange moved
in other directions as well. Growing trade
and imperialism brought increased awareness of societies in Asia and Africa to the
West. European imperialists were often
dismissive of these societies, proclaiming
their great backwardness. But artists often
had a different appreciation, and the new
contacts had significant influence on Western art.

Fruitful exchanges of artistic styles have
been common in world history; we have seen
the impact of Buddhism on Chinese art, and
of Greece on Indian art. In this sense, the
modern exchange between Africa and Asia,
on the one hand, and Europe, on the other,
was part of a well-established pattern. The
exchange was somewhat unexpected, however, given Europeans' sense of superiority
in most cultural matters. Even in art, where
Europe borrowed heavily in the creation of
its modern styles, the power imbalance was
reflected in the use of such terms as "tradi-

tional" or "primitive" in describing rich traditions in Africa and Asia.

Exhibitions of African art proliferated as
part of the returns of imperialism in the
early decades of the twentieth century.
Many European artists took note of the dramatic, spare lines of traditional West
African sculpture and wood- and metalwork.
Another set of inspirations came from
Japan after it was opened to Western contact following 1853. Many European artists
welcomed Japanese use of color and the
stylized forms of design—echoed also in
Chinese art.

These distinctive renditions of nature and
individuals became available at a time when
many European artists were seeking alternatives to traditional Western representa-
tional styles. Intellectual movements that
vaunted defiance of tradition in the name of
individual expression and a more venture-
some art undergirded this revolutionary current in the arts. The rise of photography
also helped convince artists that something

Influence of Asia and Africa in the Western Arts 19th and 20th Centuries

- - - ▸ *Trade routes between Asia, Africa, Europe, and U.S. (1853–1900)*

▪ *Areas of artistic influence*

▪ *Countries influenced by African and Asian art*

North Sea

Baltic
Sea

Sea of Okhotsk

Vincent van Gogh

NETHERLANDS

*North
Atlantic
Ocean*

Matisse
*Surrealism
Art Nouveau
Symbolism
Impresionism*

FRANCE

Caspian
Sea

Aral
Sea

SPAIN

Black Sea

JAPAN

to U.S.

Pablo Picasso

Mediterranean Sea

**Frank
Lloyd
Wright**

*Islamic
designs*

MOROCCO
(French)

Persian
Gulf

*Use of color &
stylized forms
of design*

Gulf of
Oman

*Woodcuts &
prints*

*Statues, masks,
sculpture, wood,
and metal work*

Red
Sea

Architecture

GAMBIA
(British)

FRENCH WEST AFRICA

Bay
of Bengal

Arabian
Sea

South China
Sea

PORTUGUESE
GUINEA

SIERRA
LEONE
(British)

NIGERIA
(British)

Andaman
Sea

LIBERIA

Gulf of
Thailand

GOLD COAST
(British)

TOGO
(German)

CAMEROONS
(German)

to Polynesia

RIO MUNI
(Spain)

FRENCH
EQUATORIAL
AFRICA

BELGIAN
CONGO

Indian Ocean

Java Sea

ANGOLA
(Portuguese)

Arafura
Sea

Timor Sea

Coral Sea

*South
Atlantic
Ocean*

*Great
Australian Bight*

Primitivism
Paul Gauguin

Tahiti

POLYNESIA
(French)

beyond literal portrayals was essential in painting and other visual arts. Non-European influences both stimulated and guided this general movement.

One pace-setting French artist, Paul Gauguin, carried his quest for non-Western inspiration to the Pacific islands, where he spent the latter part of his career. Gauguin's work, featuring native peoples and landscapes and showing the influence of Polynesian styles, had significant impact on artistic innovation in Europe. Other artists followed imperialism to other settings, such as North Africa and the Middle East; here, however, the result often involved exotic themes rather than stylistic impact, though some individual artists, like Henri Matisse, were deeply influenced by Islamic designs.

The surge of Japanese imports to the West after 1853 introduced Japanese art pieces, mainly in the form of woodcuts and prints. There were many exhibitions held in Western Europe, where the public and artists alike admired this foreign art. Both traditional (seventeenth- and eighteenth-century work) and contemporary art won attention. Many books about the nature of Japanese art were published during the 1870s, and by 1890 Japanese art had become an integral part of the modern art movements. The first form of art to be influenced by Japanese art was painting. For the impressionists in Europe, Japanese art meant liberation from the rigid rules of classical painting, which were being taught at academies. Japanese paintings were simple, consisting of objects and themes in nature. Woodblock prints were even more influential in their emphasis on simple, graceful designs. Instead of the ceremonial, religious themes of classical art, Japanese art recognized the artistic value of natural posture. The depth of Japanese paintings and prints, which forced the eye to concentrate in the middle and background, was hailed as revolutionary. In response, Impressionists focused on plants, animals, and simple things, such as buildings, bridges, or boats on a river. Depictions of animals foreign to the European continent were also encouraged by Japanese art objects. Tigers and other "exotic" animals became the theme of many artists, who imitated Japanese art. In a way, Japanese art, combined with other Eastern influences, brought a love for nature and simplicity to a heavily industrialized Europe. But Japanese urban themes also won attention, as in the street-life scenes of Hiroshige.

The influence of Japanese art continued during the twentieth century. Art Nouveau, which came into being during the First World War, was heavily influenced by Japanese art. Followers of Art Nouveau, Symbolism, and Surrealism all experimented with Japanese art, its themes and concepts. For example, Art Nouveau artists created works that are long and thin, shaped after Japanese scrolls. Japanese influences also contributed to the formation of posters as art objects. Japanese art is commonly accepted as the basis for abstract art. The religious, inner-peace motivations behind Japanese art were replaced by a remote reality. Japanese architecture also had a profound impact on modern Western architecture. The high functionality of the Japanese house, with its sliding doors, veil-like walls, and rectangular base design, were adapted by the architects of both Art Nouveau and the modern movement. Frank Lloyd Wright and other architects of the twentieth century stressed modularity and adaptability of the Japanese house, which was designed to make additions easier. Japanese art became the stepping-stone of Western art as it made the leap between classical and modern traditions.

African art came to Europe well after Asian and Japanese arts were introduced. Individual African art pieces were imported, capturing the imagination of some of the greatest artists of the early twentieth century. Almost all of the African art objects imported to Europe were statuettes and masks. Led by Matisse and Pablo Picasso, some artists came to reject the classical concept of "beauty is truth, truth beauty." The primitive-looking faces of African statuettes and

Vincent van Gogh
Olive Trees at Montmajour
(July, 1888)
Musée des Beaux-Arts, Tournai, Belgium
Scala/Art Resource

Ike Taiga
The Gathering at the Orchid Pavillion
Property of Mary Griggs Burke
Photograph by Kazumasa Ichikawa

masks came to represent this rejection of beauty. Just like the Impressionists, who tried to break the bondage of classical art with Japanese influences, these artists used African statuettes and masks to break the classical conception of beauty in art. There were other reasons for the strong influence of African art. The simplicity of the statuettes and masks appealed to artists for the same reasons that Japanese woodcuts appealed to the Impressionists: they reminded artists of older contacts with nature.

The person responsible for introducing Oceanic art to Europe is Paul Gauguin (1848–1904). After losing his job as a stockbroker and trying unsuccessfully to sell his art in Europe, Gauguin came to dislike the civilization and art there. He settled in Tahiti and explored the art form called Primitivism, which in his hands involved a combination of Polynesian masks and statuettes. Gauguin declared his admiration for primitive art as follows: "Primitive Art proceeds from the spirit and makes use of nature. The so-called refined art proceeds from sensuality and serves nature. Nature is the servant of the former and the mistress of the latter. She demeans man's spirit by allowing him to adore her. This is the way that we tumbled into the abominable error of naturalism."

Conclusion

The long-term result of these vigorous exchanges was not a European conversion to African or Asian styles but rather the construction of a new movement of modern art that freed Western painting and design from conventional constraints. Use of color in Impressionism, and use of shapes in other movements, such as Cubism, became the framework for the innovative modern art that would continue through the twentieth century. Pablo Picasso, the most famous twentieth-century artist, was heavily influenced by his acquaintance with African masks and other art forms throughout his long and varied career.

Western artistic interests, at both the creative and the more popular levels, would influence other traditions in turn, thanks to the powerful position of Europe in the contemporary world. Modern art styles, from Impressionism to more abstract renderings, won important participation in Latin America, the United States, and Japan, where painters worked in the new modes though sometimes intertwined older themes as well. A true international style took shape, setting the groundwork for some of the most important art of the twentieth century. At the same time, Western tourists helped inspire modifications to traditional art in places like Africa, where older styles were modified to appeal to Western taste and the possibilities of mass production.

The emergence of an international style had one final effect: the commitment of artists in some societies, like India and much of the Middle East, to traditional styles as a statement of identity against the cosmopolitan mode. And some societies, like communist China and Russia, attempted to produce styles, in the fashion called "socialist realism," that were neither purely traditional nor international, with leaders regarding the abstractions of modern art decadent and unprogressive. While international styles have advanced in the twentieth century, they have also generated important reactions and exceptions.

Suggested Readings

Roland Penrose, *Picasso, His Life and Work* (Berkeley, 1981); Judy Sund, *True to Temperament: Van Gogh and French Naturalist Literature* (New York, 1992); David Sweetman, *Paul Gauguin: A Life* (New York, 1995); Siegfried Wichmann, *Japonisme: The Japanese Influence on Western Art in the Nineteenth and Twentieth Centuries* (New York, 1981).

13. The Spread of Marxism

Marxism is a political and economic philosophy that developed in Western Europe in the middle of the nineteenth century. Karl Marx himself, a German who spent most of his adult life in England, along with many followers, worked to use Marxism's complex yet appealing theories to generate a mass movement. By persuasion, example, and force—a familiar combination in the spread of cultural systems—Marxism did win massive numbers of followers in many parts of the world, from the 1860s into the later twentieth century. Marxism's diffusion resembles that of many world religions in providing intense beliefs that could capture the minds and guide the behavior of people in many otherwise different societies. Although fading at the end of the twentieth century, Marxism unquestionably counts as one of the key belief systems of contemporary world history.

"Workers of the world, unite! You have nothing to lose but your chains," wrote Marx. Beginning with the "Communist Manifesto" of 1848, he argued that the history of the world has been a history of class struggle and of oppression by the class that owned the basic means of production over those who did the work that produced goods of value. Earlier phases of the struggle had revolved around slavery and then manorialism (which Marx called feudalism). The latter struggle had given rise to the dominant, capitalistic middle class. Marx saw the spreading Industrial Revolution as redefining class struggle. The oppressor was now the bourgeoisie, the capitalists who oppressed the working class, or proletariat, in order to win profits. Capitalism bent every aspect of society—government, art, even the treatment of women—to the demands of its system. Capitalism also steadily expanded the proletariat by driving small owners out of business while increasing worker misery. Here, however, were the seeds of its destruction, for an expanding working class would organize and overthrow the bourgeoisie by violent revolution. Workers would unite internationally, for national boundaries were simply products of capitalism. Through revolution they would seize the state and form a temporary dictatorship that would remove all vestiges of capitalism and the capitalists.

Spread of Marxist Ideology

■ *Areas where Marxist ideology spread in its original form, usually among workers and some middle-class members in industrial countries*

■ *Areas where Marxist ideology spread among workers, farmers, and key political leaders, in peasant-based societies*

■ *Areas where Marxist ideology spread among some protest leaders but did not widely influence workers or peasants*

■ *Areas where Marxist ideology was introduced through external force*

Beaufort Sea

Greenland Sea

Baffin Bay

Norwegian Sea

Gulf of Alaska

Hudson Bay

Labrador Sea

Sea of Okhotsk

North
Pacific
Ocean

North
Atlantic Ocean

North Sea

Baltic
Sea

English Channel

Sea of
Japan

Gulf of Mexico

Bay of Biscay

Black Sea

Caspian
Sea

Aral
Sea

East
China
Sea

Caribbean Sea

Mediterranean Sea

Persian
Gulf

Gulf of
Oman

Arabian
Sea

Bay
of Bengal

South China
Sea

Philippine Sea

Pacific Ocean

Red
Sea

Gulf of Aden

Andaman
Sea

Gulf of
Thailand

Indian Ocean

Java Sea

Arafura
Sea

Timor Sea

Coral Sea

South
Pacific Ocean

South
Atlantic Ocean

Great
Australian Bight

Tasman
Sea

Thus purified, society would then move toward a durable perfection. All people would be treated fairly, including women, who would no longer be oppressed by institutions like prostitution. The state would wither away, for there would be no need for force to keep an unjust system in power. People would spontaneously produce what they could and consume what they needed, as private property would be abolished. Religion and other deceptive cultural snares would be driven out. Marx firmly believed in the power of science and technology and assumed that these would work for the good in a revolutionized society.

Marxism had great appeal. It could inspire educated people from any social class who were looking for a system to explain current injustice and guide action. It was a tailor-made ideology for revolutionaries, for it told them that revolution was essential and inevitable, but also that it would win, backed by the force of history. Marxism readily appealed to many urban and rural workers eager to throw off current oppression and look toward a more perfect future, in which their labor would be rewarding and free. Marxism also attracted people concerned about colonial or racial oppression who could link Marx's attack on capitalism, and his revolutionary remedies and solutions, to their own desire for freedom. Because it supported science and industrial advances

without accepting the current social and political systems of the West, Marxism could combine the desire for modern progress with the quest for justice—in a number of different parts of the world.

Marx himself was an intellectual, but he eagerly taught his theories to a number of other theorists and labor leaders from several countries, many of whom sought refuge in liberal England. From this nucleus, Marxist labor movements—both unions and political parties—began to fan out in various parts of Europe from the 1860s onward. From European movements, in turn, emigrants brought Marxism to many parts of the Americas, aided by the power and dissemination of Marxist writings. A Marxist International organization loosely linked labor movements across national lines. Marxism's solid European base inspired a number of Russian radicals who were eager to embrace an established doctrine that could help them unseat the tsarist regime. Here and elsewhere, Marxism profited from its Western origins—it shared the cultural prestige of the West as the world's most advanced industrial society—while also providing ideas that were opposed to dominant Western modes. Russian Marxism helped spur the Russian revolutions of the early twentieth century, and Lenin, a convinced Marxist, quickly took charge of the 1917 revolution, providing the world's first Marx-

ist government. By this point radical students from various parts of the world, particularly Asia, were picking up Marxism in their studies in the West and in the Soviet Union, generating Marxist intellectual activity and labor agitation in a number of areas. The Soviet government, ardently Marxist, spread Marxist ideas internally in its expanding school systems while endorsing efforts to promote the doctrine in all corners of the world. Convinced of its justice, the Soviets also used force to spread Marxism to parts of central Asia under their control, and later, after World War II, to most of Eastern Europe. As the Soviet Union became a superpower, providing an example of successful industrialization and an alternative to Western capitalism and colonialism, and explicitly educating potential leaders from all parts of the world, Marxism spread still more widely during the 1950s and 1960s.

Marxism was no hollow belief system used simply to justify the ambition of a few revolutionaries or the national interests of the Russian state. Many people converted to Marxism even when they encountered it through compulsory school systems or through propaganda campaigns. Marxism could explain what the world was like, and certainly what society should be. It provided clear enemies, in capitalism and, often, the capitalist West. It came to support particular kinds of artistic movements, like Socialist

Realism, bent on glorifying workers. Marxism even developed holidays and rituals, such as the international May Day, to celebrate the power of labor in most parts of the world (though sedulously avoided by the United States, which designated a different date and non-Marxist imagery for its Labor Day).

As Marxism spread, it also changed and adapted, like all successful international cultural movements. Changes varied from reformism to more focused revolutionary efforts. Many Western Europeans came by the 1890s to modify Marxism with a belief that labor progress might come peacefully through major but gradual reforms; this kind of Marxism, blasted by purists, was called revisionism, and it long guided most European socialist movements—even ones that insisted on Marxist purity in principle. Communist parties, springing into being after the Russian Revolution, normally maintained a purer revolutionary stance, though they too could sometimes think in terms of a reformist approach. Russian leaders explicitly adapted Marxism to their situation. Lenin provided a vital theoretical addition to the intellectual system by arguing that international capitalism had now spread worldwide; hence even a country like the Soviet Union, without a big internal capitalist class, could have a proletarian rebellion that would lead to the communist

utopia. Lenin also emphasized the importance of a vanguard communist party in leading the revolution. Stalin, the leader of the Soviet Union by the late 1920s, combined Marxism-Leninism with a vigorous dose of nationalism, arguing that the Soviet state could go it alone in a hostile world— even though nationalism was technically anathema to Marxist theory. Marxist leaders in China explicitly adjusted Marxism to appeal to peasants, arguing that revolution would free peasants from landlord control. For Mao Zedong, peasants substituted for proletariat as the class capable of revolution. In Cuba, Fidel Castro and Che Guevara stressed rural guerrilla warfare as the means of revolution. In various places, Marxists sometimes compromised with existing religions, allowing people to practice their faith despite the theoretical incompatibility with Marxist attacks on religion as the "opiate of the masses."

Marxism spread in various ways and at various times. Three patterns predominated. Marx himself, and most of his immediate followers, were particularly interested in dissemination to labor leaders, ordinary workers, and revolutionaries of various backgrounds in the industrial countries. Here, according to the theory, was where revolution would first occur. Marxism gained many converts—some intensely devoted, others convinced but a bit more casual—in a number of industrial areas, mainly through propaganda, shared writings, contacts at international meetings, and the power of example. There was important variety: Britain and Scandinavia did not produce big Marxist groups, for the dominant labor movements, though influenced by Marxist ideas and individual leaders, favored a non-Marxist socialism. The same was true in North America, where Marxist beliefs had some influence but won no massive conversions. Marxist diffusion was much more important in France, Italy, Germany (until suppressed by Hitler), East-Central Europe, Australia, Argentina, Chile, and Japan. Many movements, some of them successful in winning a share in government, and many workers and intellectuals (and sometimes peasant groups) embraced Marxist ideas. Russia, though newly industrializing in about 1900, fell largely into this category of Marxist diffusion.

A second pattern of diffusion involved largely non-industrial societies with a strong peasant presence, in which Marxist converts, often initially trained in the West, worked hard to persuade the masses, and other revolutionary leaders, of the truth of their system. Usually, Marxism in these cases was combined with an urgent desire to remove colonial or Western-oriented regimes, as well as to combat large landholders and other traditional sources of inequality. Some societies, again, remained largely immune, particularly where strong religions held mass allegiance. Thus Marxism, while winning a few supporters, made few inroads in the Muslim world or West Africa or in some parts of Latin America.

A third pattern involved outright force. Marxist revolutions in Russia, China, and Cuba resulted in part from diffusion of the first or second type. But once revolutionaries were successful, they actively attacked other cultural systems, including religion, and used education and the police to press Marxist beliefs on the rest of the population—with some, though incomplete, success. Marxist conquest also brought Marxism to additional territories. Consolidation of the revolution in Russia brought Marxism to central Asia on the heels of the Red Army. Post–World War II Soviet expansion drove Marxist regimes to power throughout East-Central Europe, including East Germany (though there were important local Marxist groups already on the ground as a result of earlier conversions and diffusion). A 1970s war brought a Marxist system to Afghanistan. Chinese expansion brought Marxist control to Tibet. Soviet and Chinese influence alike helped spread Marxism to North Korea and Vietnam, though, particularly in Vietnam, local revolutionary agitation had already created an important Marxist base.

Marxism began to recede, though not to disappear, after the 1970s. Heavy-handed Soviet policies antagonized some Marxists in the West, while growing prosperity reduced worker interest in Marxism. Then at the end of the 1980s the Soviet system collapsed. Most of central Asia (including Afghanistan) and Eastern Europe cast off Marxist systems and moved toward religious, consumerist, or other cultural orientations. In much of communist Asia, Marxism retained a greater hold, but the introduction of market mechanisms reduced its influence over the economy. Many Marxists kept the faith, or some version of the faith, even in countries were the communist state had been overthrown. The future of this exceptionally powerful cultural force was not entirely clear, even as its lights dimmed during the 1990s.

Europe and North America

Marxism initially spread in Europe and North America through the influence of writings by Marx and his immediate followers, through propaganda efforts by Marxist international leadership, and through the active mobility of many workers and radical agitators. Many workers traveled back and forth—for example, from Italy to France or the United States around 1900—and they could easily carry ideas with them. Extensive Marxism did not necessarily re-

Democratically elected Marxist government

Marxist government that came to power by revolution

Marxist government installed by a foreign power

Marxist government that came to power through foreign military and political pressure

Estonia, Latvia,
Lithuania,
1945–1990

Belarus, Ukraine,
Moldova, Russia,
1917–1990

GDR, Poland,
Czechoslovakia,
Hungary,
1946–1990

Kazakhstan, Uzbekistan,
Kyrgyzstan, Tajikistan,
Turkmenistan,
1923–1990

Mongolia,
1945–1990

Yugoslavia,
Albania,
1945–1991

China,
1948–present

North Korea,
1945–present

Romania,
Bulgaria,
1946–1991

Georgia,
Armenia,
Azerbaijan,
1920–1990

Afghanistan,
1979–1989

North
Atlantic Ocean

North
Pacific
Ocean

Cuba,
1959–present

Vietnam,
1956–present

Pacific Ocean

Nicaragua,
1979–1990

Kampuchea,
1975–1979

Ethiopia,
1975–1991

Indian Ocean

Tanzania,
1977–1985

Angola,
1975–1991

Madagascar,
1977–1992

Mozambique,
1975–1990

South
Pacific Ocean

Chile,
1970–1973

South
Atlantic Ocean

sult—the greatest conversions occurred in such places as France, Germany, and Belgium—but everywhere in these regions Marxist ideas and individual leaders had measurable influence, despite efforts at official repression.

Marxism spread into Eastern Europe in a similar fashion. Russia, Czechoslovakia, Hungary, and Poland all began industrialization by the late nineteenth century. All had active intellectual contacts with the West. In many cases, local radicals might be exiled to the West—as was Lenin, who spent time in Switzerland. Skilled workers were brought in from more established industrial areas, another source of cultural influence. Significant Marxist political movements developed. But these important beginnings were then supplemented by force and example—the power of the 1917 revolution in Russia, Ukraine, and elsewhere (which also added to the influence of Marxism beyond Soviet borders), and then conquest by Russian armies and subsequent occupation during and after World War II. Marxist movements were small in Yugoslavia and Albania before the war, but they gained power in resistance to Nazism, appealing to nationalists and peasants; here was a basis for postwar Marxist regimes without much Soviet interference. The Red Army forced Marxism on Bulgaria and Romania, which had remained relatively free of Marxist thinking. A similar pattern existed in the Baltic states, where only small movements existed prior to the Soviet invasion as part of World War II.

Asia, Africa, and Latin America

Marxism exhibited several patterns in Asia. The spread of ideas affected radical leaders and many workers in Japan by 1900, as an important part of Western cultural and economic contacts more generally and as an outgrowth of the tensions produced by rapid industrialization. This was only a minority current, however, often fiercely attacked by the government.

Marxism in central Asia spread after communist victory in Russia as Red armies swept through this region, formerly mostly part of tsarist Russia, during the 1920s. None had developed significant Marxism prior to the effects of Marxist takeover by force. This pattern also briefly applied, later on, to Afghanistan. Soviet pressure (though not outright force) also promoted a Marxist regime in Mongolia.

Spurred by some English propagandists, a group of English-educated Indian Marxists sprang up, linked to the growing nationalist movement in the early twentieth century. Marxism was not dominant at the national level, though it influenced the thinking of leaders like Gandhi and Nehru, but it gained considerable power in a few states. Here was a case of voluntary appeal in a largely non-industrial society. Similar patterns existed in Indonesia, where Dutch Marxists imported the ideas before World War I and helped the formation of a Marxist party. Marxism contributed to independence efforts but never gained a large role.

China was the seat of Marxism's greatest triumph in Asia. The ideas arrived soon after World War I, as the new Soviet revolutionary regime began promoting a movement. Early Marxist leaders were students and activists educated in the Soviet Union, Germany, and France. Led particularly by Mao Zedong, a powerful leader who was not educated abroad, Chinese Marxists quickly moved to woo the peasantry, promising land reform, and became linked to nationalist interests in opposing Western and Japanese influence. Maoism also added to Marxism, at points, a desire to industrialize through small production centers rather than factories; it also explicitly attacked Confucianism, with its belief in elitist education and the prestige of traditional culture. Adaptations of this sort, combined with effective military strategies, put Marxists in control of the country soon after World War II.

Marxism spread to Vietnam and other parts of Indochina through contact with France.

Many Vietnamese served as soldiers in France during World War I, others as workers; and some brought communist ideas back with them. Ho Chi Minh, who had worked as a waiter in Paris, combined Marxism with anticolonial nationalism and a genius in guerrilla warfare. More than Mao, in part because of greater European influence, Ho advocated industrialization and limited the adaptation to peasant goals.

Marxism spread to Korea from the Soviet Union during the 1920s, in resistance to Japanese occupation. Several future leaders were educated in the Soviet Union; they gained control over North Korea, backed by the Red Army, after World War II. Marxism came to Malaysia from China in the 1930s, linked to nationalism and the trade unions. After a guerrilla movement in 1948 was put down by the British, Marxism declined.

Marxism followed three patterns in Latin America. In some areas it gained little influence. In several industrial countries, notably Chile and Argentina, Marxism won significant political power in association with working-class groups. It spread initially through the immigration of European workers and exiled leaders (some of whom, from France and Germany, had participated in the revolutions of 1848). By the early twentieth century, working classes were large enough to provide a significant social base, and significant Marxist parties developed by the 1920s. Repression pushed back Marxism in Argentina in the 1960s, and in Chile a Marxist election victory in 1970 was reversed by a military coup in 1973, leading to systematic police attacks.

Marxism in some other parts of Latin America came later, thanks to propaganda and other activities sponsored by the Soviet Union and to a lesser extent China. Leaders were trained abroad (or, after 1959, in Cuba). Marxism appealed to peasants and Indian groups in Peru, Nicaragua, Guatemala, El Salvador, and Colombia (a major movement arose in Peru as late as the 1980s). The Cuban revolution combined peasant and middle-class dissident support for a Marxist movement; similarly, Mexican Marxism, a significant force up to the 1940s, combined labor movement and peasant support. Overall, however, most Marxist success in Central America, the Andes, and the Caribbean reflected both outside sponsorship and significant adaptation to peasant interests.

Marxism reached parts of sub-Saharan Africa extensively in the 1950s, in association with nationalist efforts against colonialism. Some Africans learned of Marxism through periods of schooling abroad. Then, however, Marxism was blended with nationalist and pan-African ideals, though there was little impact on mass beliefs. Key leaders in eastern and southern Africa were guided by the adapted Marxism, trying to combine it with the traditional communal interactions of African rural society. A few Marxist-led revolts occurred, notably in Ethiopia, where a Soviet authoritarian model prevailed for a time. South Africa constituted a distinctive case. Marxism developed from 1906, thanks to greater European influence and the arrival of English-speaking industrial workers. Marxism helped shape leadership in the African National Congress, which opposed racial segregation and oppression, including the nation's first democratically elected president, Nelson Mandela. Even with somewhat greater influence, Marxism in South Africa gained no role as a mass cultural movement.

Conclusion

The extraordinary spread of Marxism, over more than a century, testified to the power of this cultural system and the diverse needs to which it could respond. It also showed the new speed of international movement and communication, capable of propelling even a feared protest ideology across cultural borders. These two factors explain why Marxism followed geographical patterns of cultural connection never before seen in world history. Like all cultural contacts, however, Marxism's spread was diverse and uneven. So, at the end of the twentieth century, was its apparent retreat. The ideology still influenced leaders and intellectuals in many parts of the world, with important mass adherence in key sections of Asia and in Cuba, and with a potential for revival elsewhere.

Suggested Readings

Alex Callincos, *The Revenge of History: Marxism and the East European Revolutions* (University Park, Pa., 1991); A. Dirlik, *The Origins of Chinese Communism* (Oxford, 1989); Sheila Fitzpatrick, *The Russian Revolution, 1917–1932* (New York, 1982); William Friedland, ed., *African Socialism* (Stanford, 1964); D. McLellan, *Karl Marx: His Life and Thought* (New York, 1974); M. Meisner, *Mao's China, and After: A History of the People's Republic* (New York, 1986); Gary Steenson, *After Marx, Before Lenin: Marxism and Socialist Working-Class Parties in Europe, 1884–1914* (Pittsburgh, 1991).

14. International Consumer Culture

The spread of consumer products and related values was one of the key developments in twentieth-century world history. I focus here on three specific disseminations: the spread of British sports in the later nineteenth century, supplementing or displacing traditional games in many parts of the world; the development of Hollywood as an international entertainment center; and the recent global success of American-based fast-food chains, supplementing and challenging traditional eating habits in many areas.

A shared popular culture, based on common attraction to consumer products and entertainments, including sports, had several components. European and American influence spread through imperialism—the Japanese learned baseball in the 1890s from American sailors pressing American goods and military might in the Pacific. More rapid communication and transportation systems facilitated common consumer knowledge; by the late twentieth century many Israeli, Turkish, and American teenagers could readily talk (in English) about the same set of movie and rock stars, based on hours of ardent viewing of MTV and reading of fan magazines. Tens of thousands of Asians and Africans studying and working in Europe and the United States formed another link in the chain of cultural influence. And of course explicit efforts by commercial companies to sell products, invoking the prestige of Western standards of living, did further work. American cigarette companies pushed their wares in Asia amid a backdrop of cowboys—international icons of masculine chic. An international symbolic language even more widespread than English was developing based on Western-style popular and consumer culture.

The same developments provoked diverse, often fierce, resistance. Nationalists like India's Gandhi blasted Western shallowness and materialism; his vision of India was simpler and purer. Communists, at least until the 1970s, defined prosperity in different terms and sought (unsuccessfully) to insulate their societies from Western consumer goods and media (though they adopted international sports with a vengeance). Reli-

Hollywood, McDonald's, and Soccer: The Spread of International Consumer Culture

‑ ‑ ‑ ► *Spread of soccer*

▬ ▬ ► *Spread of McDonald's*

▬▬▬► *Spread of American film industry*

Greenland Sea

Beaufort Sea

Baffin Bay

Norwegian Sea

Gulf of Alaska

Hudson Bay

Labrador Sea

CANADA
*First McDonald's
1967*

BRITAIN
*Birth of
soccer 1845*

SOVIET UNION
*First McDonald's
1990*

Sea of Okhotsk

PARIS & LONDON
*American film
companies open
foreign
branches 1896*

EUROPE

ILLINOIS
*McDonald's first
restaurant 1955*

WESTERN EUROPE
*First McDonald's
1971–1992*

*Caspian
Sea*

*Aral
Sea*

Black Sea

LOS ANGELES
*American film
companies establish
foreign branches
1916–1918*

Gulf of Mexico

PUERTO RICO
*First McDonald's
1967*

MORROCO
*First McDonald's
1992*

Mediterranean Sea

*Sea of
Japan*

JAPAN *First McDonald's
1971*

*East
China
Sea*

*Red
Sea*

*Gulf of
Oman*

INDIA

*Bay
of Bengal*

*South China
Sea*

Philippine Sea

VENEZUELA
*American film
rights bought in 1867*

LATIN AMERICA
*Soccer spread
in the 1890s*

Gulf of Aden

*Arabian
Sea*

*Andaman
Sea*

SINGAPORE

*Gulf of
Thailand*

Indian Ocean

Pacific Ocean

BRAZIL

AFRICA
*Soccer spread
1910–1940*

INDONESIA

*Arafura
Sea*

BRAZIL
*First McDonald's
1979*

*Timor
Sea*

Coral Sea

LATIN AMERICA

*South
Atlantic
Ocean*

URUGUAY

CHILE   ARGENTINA

*First McDonald's
1971*
AUSTRALIA

*South
Pacific Ocean*

*Great
Australian Bight*

*Tasman
Sea*

SOUTH AFRICA
*American and French
films shown in 1910*

NEW ZEALAND
*First McDonald's
1971*

gious leaders attacked Western goods as false gods, often associating them with excessive sexuality and other immoralities. The Islamic revivals of the 1970s frequently focused on rejecting Western consumer patterns, including imported films, and restoring more traditional entertainments and gender standards. It was not clear that Western-sponsored consumerism would win out uniformly.

The first popular-cultural influence to spread from the West, beginning in the second half of the nineteenth century, involved new sports. Sports were gaining ground in Europe and the United States at this point. Most had origins in traditional popular games, but in the nineteenth century they were regularized, given set rules (and often referees), and commercialized, with new products and, quickly, professional teams. The most important sport, originating in Britain, proved to be soccer, whose rules were codified in 1845. Spreading rapidly in Britain, soccer became a sport with wide working-class as well as upper-class participation and, by the 1870s, successful professional teams. It spread rapidly in Europe, by children studying in English schools and through British sailors and factory managers, and then began to move beyond Western borders. European diplomatic and business personnel, including factory managers, set up local teams in many Latin American port cities. The first Buenos Aires soccer club was copied from local British residents in 1867, and a national network of teams fanned out by the 1890s. British sailors began playing soccer in Rio de Janeiro in 1884, and the son of an English diplomat set up local clubs from 1894 onward. By 1898 Mackenzie College had a mostly Brazilian team, and in 1902 a full league was set up around São Paolo. As in England, Brazilian soccer started amid upper-class popularity, spurred by the prestige of British culture, but then spread rapidly among the lower classes. Patterns in Chile, Uruguay, and elsewhere were similar. The first intracontinental match, between Uruguay and Argentina, occurred in 1902, and by 1916, Chile and Argentina had joined the international soccer federation. Later in the twentieth century Latin American teams regularly competed for top spots in World Cup competitions, the most widely watched sports events worldwide.

As the movie industry developed in the early twentieth century, exports quickly became an important component. Venezuela bought American film rights as early as 1896. American film companies set up direct foreign branches in London and Paris, also in 1896. American and French films were being shown in South Africa in 1910. The big move occurred during World War I, when Universal Studios opened branches in Japan, India, Singapore, and Indonesia—by 1918, Universal had twenty foreign branches in all. Twentieth Century Fox spread to Canada, Latin America, and Australia, as well as to Europe, in the same period. By the early 1920s American films controlled 95 percent of the Australian market. Americans were seen as holding the secret to making films that appealed to the masses, and budding European companies were held back during World War I at a crucial development point. Hollywood became the international movie capital, shaper of international images of beauty and sexuality. By the late 1970s films and television shows constituted the second most important American export (after aircraft).

Another development, more subtle, formed a familiar part of international cultural contact. Many societies received Western consumer influence but added their own components. A craze for American-style game shows in Japan was given a distinctive twist: losing contestants were elaborately shamed, subjected to ridicule to highlight their failure to live up to group norms—thus serving Japanese cultural goals in ways that would seem harsh to more individualistic Americans. Comic books, imported as a genre into Mexico in the 1930s, quickly took on Mexican themes, as Mexican heroes beat gringo stars such as Superman, bandits who shared with the poor were glorified as anti-capitalists, and kinship and family ties received greater attention.

McDonald's opened its first restaurant, in Illinois, in 1955, building on the example of smaller fast-food chains. The company catered to traditional American interest in eating fast, adding a family atmosphere and typical American food products. International expansion came quickly, to Canada and Puerto Rico in 1967. From that point until 1988, the corporation entered an average of two new countries a year, and then speeded up in the 1990s. By 1998 it operated in 109 countries overall. Western Europe, New Zealand, and Australia were obvious targets, though McDonald's and its American companions surprised observers with their success in traditional centers of gourmet cuisine, like France. The company found quick success in Japan, where it won its largest foreign audience; "Makadonaldo" opened in the world-famous Ginza, in Tokyo, in 1971. McDonald's entry into the Soviet Union, in 1990, was a major sign of the ending of Cold War rivalries and the growing Russian passion for Western consumer goods; the restaurant, which had to organize special training to create smiling personnel, won massive patronage despite (by Russian standards) very high prices.

The triumph of Western leisure and consumer forms constitutes one of the great stories of cultural contact, often bemoaned by observers who worry about the triteness of Western popular culture and the loss of vital diversity worldwide. Yet the story remains complex. Even McDonald's has not penetrated everywhere. Argentineans adopted soccer, but they added a more individualistic, exuberant playing style, compared with the restrained, team-minded British. Sports diversity reminds us of the ongoing importance of regional variety: India and Pakistan, open to much Western influence, did not surge forward as leading sports centers, their greatest success occurring not in soccer but in more individualized or upper-class ventures, such as squash and polo. McDonald's triumphed widely, but it also adapted. It developed kosher outlets in Israel, McDavid's; for Japan it developed a burger with teriyaki sauce (McTeriyaki). McDonald's also adjusted to Indian traditions by expanding its vegetarian offerings, but, despite the country's huge population, it was able to establish only a handful of outlets—the company's international appeal was far from uniform. Even Hollywood's triumphs remain uneven. Indians watch some foreign films, but as the world's largest center of film production India concentrates more on movies based on its own epic stories, which do not export widely. Hong Kong for a time was a major film production center for Asia. Egypt and Russia are two other major film centers catering to regional demand. How far international cultural homogenization will go, what gains and losses it will entail, remain unanswered questions.

Suggested Readings

Ian Jarvie, *Hollywood's Overseas Campaign: The North Atlantic Movie Trade, 1920–1950* (Cambridge, Eng., 1996); Janet Lever, *Soccer Madness* (Chicago, 1983); Kerry Seagrave, *American Films Abroad: Hollywood's Domination of the World's Movie Screens from the 1890s to the Present* (Jefferson, N.C., 1997); Theodore von Laue, *The World Revolution of Westernization: The Twentieth Century in Global Perspective* (New York, 1987); James Watson, ed., *Golden Arches East: McDonald's in East Asia* (Stanford, 1998); www.mcdonalds.com.

Bibliography

Chapter 1

Martin Bernal, *Black Athena: The Afroasiatic Roots of Classical Civilization* (New Brunswick, N.J., 1987); Walter Burkert, *The Orientalizing Revolution: Near Eastern Influence on Greek Culture in the Early Archaic Age* (Cambridge, Mass., 1992); Arthur Cotterell, ed., *The Penguin Encyclopedia of Classical Civilizations* (London, 1993); M. Lefkowitz and G. Rogers, eds., *Black Athena Revisited* (Chapel Hill, N.C., 1996); Robert Morkot, *The Penguin Historical Atlas of Ancient Greece* (New York, 1996); Andrew Sherratt, *Economy and Society in Prehistoric Europe* (Princeton, N.J., 1997); Clifton E. Van Sickle, *A Political and Cultural History of the Ancient World from Prehistoric Times to the Dissolution of the Ottoman Empire in the West* (Boston, 1947).

Chapter 2

Arthur Cotterell, ed., *The Penguin Encyclopedia of Classical Civilizations* (London, 1993); Peter Green, ed., *Hellenistic History and Culture* (Berkeley, 1993); E. Rapson et al., eds., *The Cambridge History of India* (Cambridge, Eng., 1922); Hugh Rawlinson, *Intercourse Between India and the Western World, from the Earliest Times to the Fall of Rome*, 2nd ed. (Cambridge, Eng., 1926); Vincent A. Smith, *The Early History of India from 600 B.C. to the Muhammadan Conquest*, rev. S. M. Edwardes (Oxford, 1924).

Chapter 3

Jerry H. Bentley, *Old World Encounters: Cross-Cultural Exchanges and Contacts in Pre-Modern Times* (New York, 1993); N. Ross Reat, *Buddhism: A History* (Berkeley, 1994); Kenneth Sanders, *Epochs in Buddhist History* (Chicago, 1924); Jean Sedlar, *India and the Greek World* (Totowa, N.J., 1980); Arthur Wright, *Buddhism in Chinese History* (Stanford, 1959); Erik Zurcher, *Buddhism: Its Origin and Spread in Words, Maps, and Pictures* (New York, 1962).

Chapter 4

Gerard Chaliand, *The Penguin Atlas of Diasporas* (New York, 1995); Arnold Eisen, *Galut: Modern Jewish Reflections on Homelessness and Homecoming* (Bloomington, Ind., 1986); *Encyclopedia Judaica* (Jerusalem, 1972); Raphael Patai, *Tents of Jacob: The Diaspora, Yesterday and Today* (Englewood Cliffs, N.J., 1971); Howard Sachar, *The Course of Modern Jewish History* (New York, 1990); Howard Sachar, *Diaspora: An Inquiry into the Contemporary Jewish World* (New York, 1985).

Chapter 5

Jerry H. Bentley, *Old World Encounters* (New York, 1993); Kenneth S. Latourette, *A History of Christianity* (New York, 1953); R. A. Markus, *Christianity in the Roman World* (New York, 1974); Arno Peters, *Peters Atlas of the World* (New York, 1990).

Chapter 6

Rene Bravmann, *African Islam* (Washington, D.C., 1983); William Brice, ed., *An Historical Atlas of Islam* (Leiden, 1981); K. N. Chaudhuri, *Asia Before Europe: Economy and Civilization of the Indian Ocean from the Rise of Islam to 1750* (New York, 1990); Richard M. Eaton, *The Rise of Islam and the Bengal Frontier* (Berkeley, 1993); Mircea Eliade, ed., *The Encyclopedia of Religion* (New York, 1987); G. S. P. Freeman-Grenville, *Historical Atlas of the Middle East* (New York, 1993); J. Kritzek and W. Lewis, eds., *Islam in Africa* (New York, 1969); Ira M. Lapidus, *A History of Islamic Societies* (New York, 1988); Avril Powell, *Muslims and Missionaries in Pre-Mutiny India* (Richmond, Surrey, Eng., 1993); Francis Robinson, *Atlas of the Islamic World Since 1500* (New York, 1982); Francis Robinson, ed., *The Cambridge Illustrated History of the Islamic World* (New York, 1996); Denis Sinor, ed., *The Cambridge History of Early Inner Asia* (New York, 1990); J. Spencer Trimingham, *A History of Islam in West Africa* (London, 1962).

Chapter 7

Catherine L. Albanese, *America, Religions, and Religion* (Belmont, Calif., 1992); Kenneth S. Latourette, *A History of Christianity* (New York, 1953); Catherine Lombardi et al., *Latin American History: A Teaching Atlas* (Madison, Wis., 1983); Colin McEvedy, *The Penguin Atlas of North American History* (New York, 1988); Mark A. Noll, *A History of Christianity in the United States and Canada* (Grand Rapids, Mich., 1992); Christopher Vecsey, *On the Padre's Trail* (Notre Dame, Ind., 1996).

Chapter 8

Evgenii Anisimov, *The Reforms of Peter the Great: Progress Through Coercion in Russia*, John Alexander, trans. (Armonk, N.Y., 1993);

Carmen Blacker, *The Japanese Enlightenment: A Study of the Writings of Fukuzawa Yukichi* (Cambridge, Eng., 1964); Alfred Hall, *From Galileo to Newton, 1630 to 1720* (New York, 1982); Stuart Shapin, *The Scientific Revolution* (Chicago, 1996); P. J. Vatikiotis, *The History of Modern Egypt: From Muhammad Ali to Mubarak* (Baltimore, 1991).

Chapter 9

Margaret Butcher, *The Negro in American Culture* (New York, 1956); Gerard Chaliand, *The Penguin Atlas of Diasporas* (New York, 1995); Philip Curtin, ed., *Africa Remembered: Narratives by West Africans from the Era of the Slave Trade* (Prospect Heights, Ill., 1997); Joseph Harris, *The African Presence in Asia* (Evanston, Ill., 1971) Graham Irwin, ed., *African Abroad: A Documentary History of the Black Diaspora in Asia* (New York, 1977); Martin Kilson et al., eds., *The African Diaspora: Interpretive Essays* (Cambridge, Mass., 1976); Lawrence Levine, *Black Culture and Black Consciousness* (Oxford, 1977); George Murdock, *Africa: Its People and Their Cultural History* (New York, 1959); Jocelyn Murray, *Cultural Atlas of Africa* (New York, 1981); Ronald Segal, *The Black Diaspora* (New York, 1995); Mechal Sobel, *The World They Made Together: Black and White Values in Eighteenth-Century Virginia* (Princeton, N.J., 1987); Vincent Thompson, *The Making of the African Diaspora in the Americas* (Harlow, Essex, Eng., 1987).

Chapter 10

Benedict Anderson, *Imagined Communities: Reflections on the Origin and Spread of Nationalism* (London, 1983); J. D. Fage, *An Atlas of African History* (London, 1978); Ernest Gellner, *Nations and Nationalism* (Ithaca, N.Y., 1983); Florencia Mallon, *Peasant and Nations: The Making of Post-Colonial Mexico and Peru* (Berkeley, 1994); Hugh Seton-Watson, *Nations and States: An Enquiry into the*

Origins of Nations and the Politics of Nationalism (London, 1977); Anthony Smith, *The Ethnic Origins of Nations* (Oxford, 1986).

Chapter 11

Michael Adas, ed., *Islamic and European Expansion: The Forging of a Global Order* (Philadelphia, 1993); Ifi Amadiume, *Male Daughters, Female Husbands: Gender and Sex in an African Society* (London, 1987); Nupur Chaudhuri and Margaret Strobel, eds., *Western Women and Imperialism: Complicity and Resistance* (Bloomington, Ind., 1992); Catherine Coquery-Vidrovitch, *African Women: A Modern History* (Boulder, Colo., 1997); J. D. Fage, *An Atlas of African History* (London, 1978); Margaret Macmillan, *Women of the Raj* (London, 1988); Margaret Strobel, *Muslim Women in Mombasa, 1890-1975* (New Haven, 1979); Sjoerd de Vries, *An Atlas of World History* (London, 1965).

Chapter 12

Roland Penrose, *Picasso, His Life and Work* (Berkeley, 1981); Judy Sund, *True to Temperament: Van Gogh and French Naturalist Literature* (New York, 1992); David Sweetman, *Paul Gauguin: A Life* (New York, 1995); Siegfried Wichmann, *Japonisme: The Japanese Influence on Western Art in the Nineteenth and Twentieth Centuries* (New York, 1981).

Chapter 13

Alex Callincos, *The Revenge of History: Marxism and the East European Revolutions* (University Park, Pa., 1991); A. Dirlik, *The Origins of Chinese Communism* (Oxford, 1989); Sheila Fitzpatrick, *The Russian Revolution, 1917-1932* (New York, 1982); William Friedland, ed., *African Socialism* (Stanford, 1964); Malcolm Kennedy, *A History of Communism in East Asia* (New York, 1957); Harry Laidler, *History of Socialism: A Comparative Survey of Socialism, Communism, Trade Unionism, Cooperation, Utopianism, and Other Systems of Reform and Reconstruction* (New York, 1968); D. McLellan, *Karl Marx: His Life and Thought* (New York, 1974); M. Meisner, *Mao's China, and After: A History of the People's Republic* (New York, 1986); Thomas Nossiter, *Marxist State Governments in India: Politics, Economics, and Society* (London and Boulder, Colo., 1987); T. Skidmore and P. Smith, *Modern Latin America* (New York, 1992); Gary Steenson, *After Marx, Before Lenin: Marxism and Socialist Working-Class Parties in Europe, 1884-1914* (Pittsburgh, 1991).

Chapter 14

Ian Jarvie, *Hollywood's Overseas Campaign: The North Atlantic Movie Trade, 1920-1950* (Cambridge, Eng., 1996); Janet Lever, *Soccer Madness* (Chicago, 1983); Kerry Seagrave, *American Films Abroad: Hollywood's Domination of the World's Movie Screens from the 1890s to the Present* (Jefferson, N.C., 1997); Theodore von Laue, *The World Revolution of Westernization: The Twentieth Century in Global Perspective* (New York, 1987); James Watson, ed., *Golden Arches East: McDonald's in East Asia* (Stanford, 1998); www.mcdonalds.com.

General References Consulted

Hammond Historical Atlas of the World (Maplewood, N.J., 1995); *Rand McNally Universal World Atlas* (New York, 1991); *Santillana Atlas Historia, I: De la Edad Antigua a la Edad Moderna* (Madrid, 1999); Geoffrey Barraclough and Geoffrey Parker, *The Times Atlas of World History*, 4th ed. (Maplewood, N.J., 1993); Michael Grant, *Ancient History Atlas* (London, 1971); B. Grun and W. Stein, *The Timetables of History* (New York, 1982); H. Kinder and W. Hilgemann, *The Anchor Atlas of World History*, vols. 1 and 2, Ernest Menze, trans. (New York, 1974).

Index